Climbing to Freedom

climbs, climbers &
the climbing life

Doin' the Dog, the author near the top of Half Dome.   *photo Royal Robbins*

Climbing

to

Freedom

climbs, climbers &
the climbing life

Dick Dorworth

WESTERN EYE PRESS

2 0 1 5

CLIMBING TO FREEDOM
is published by
WESTERN EYE PRESS,
a small independent publisher
(very small, and very
independent) with a home
base in the Colorado
Rockies and an office in
Sedona Arizona.
Climbing to Freedom *is also*
available as an eBook
in various formats.

© 2015 Dick Dorworth
Western Eye Press
P O Box 1008
Sedona, Arizona 86339
1 800 333 5178
www.WesternEyePress.com

First edition, 2015
ISBN 978-0-941283-41-0

Cover
Monte Fitz Roy, Patagonia
photo
Linde Waidhofer.

Tying in *photo Susan Morning*

Contents

PART THREE: CLIMBING REFLECTIONS

PART FOUR: CLIMBING FICTION

FOREWORD

THIS IS A DIFFERENT CLIMBING BOOK. No singularity of adventure—an Everest narrative, say, or the breakthrough to an all-free ascent of the Dawn Wall. But Everest has grown moribund as a human aspiration. And even zoomed-in for live coverage, the awesome technical virtuosity of the Dawn Wall is beyond the comprehension of most of us who have devoted a lifetime to Yosemite granite. Instead, here we have a collection of pieces that probe behind the moves into the climbing experience, and its relation to our inner selves and larger lives.

The title story sets us off in a fresh and intriguing direction. We meet Elizabeth, a middle-aged woman who every summer climbs classic backcountry peaks on a pilgrimage to honor her early-teen self, clambering over the Pyrenees in a frantic bid to outrun tyranny snapping at her heels. In the Wind River Mountains of Wyoming she encounters Dick Dorworth as a young man who is neither too caught up in his own guide-like presence, nor too submersed in the tumult of life and love to appreciate her quest.

And yet the etching of this tale "took forty years," not to mention the writing of three other books—excellent ones to check out, by the way, about (one of) his other lives as a skier. All the while, however, Dorworth was mulling over Elizabeth's story: "...all those years were informed and reflected, sometime consciously, by Elizabeth's example." Finally he crystallized this meditation on freedom as (one of) the essences of climbing.

This book has been well worth the wait. Dorworth's choice of subjects, of climbs and of the often-quirky byways of climbers, is eclectic and far-flung. Yet as he roams the American West and ventures onward to some of our planet's most remote and difficult summits—probing as he goes his own motivations and joys, as well as the sometimes-shocking behavior of many ropemates—a broad range of oh-so-human themes begins to emerge.

Dick's finely honed sense of character and motivation illuminates sketches of the legendary. In many ways this is the core of the book, as we catch glimpses, through the eyes of one prominent figure after another, of what climbing is. Dick kicks this off with Royal Robbins, revealing through intense days of sharing a hard-won first ascent on the face of Half Dome—a monolith Royal had set out more or less explicitly to "own"—how this man more than any other sculpted from Yosemite granite our sense of how one should climb a rock.

It's a short step from there to Warren Harding, outwardly Royal's stylistic nemesis. We can easily see them as locked in a titanic struggle over the "ethics" of ascent and fail to notice the mutual respect behind their rather courtly sparring. Oops, I'm editorializing here. Dorworth much more wisely sticks to the unfolding of a single day where he encounters the self-described "broken-down climber." As expected, the day dawns with Harding's cynical shell, bolstered by a morning of drinking. But Dick, in a surprise move, lures old Warren out onto the rock, where we are privileged to watch as the simple act of climbing cracks that shell and leaves Warren Harding radiant.

There are many other, often short, always penetrating, glimpses of climbing's illuminati. I'm happy to say that I learned a great deal through Dick's eyes, even of people I knew well. A couple of guys whose lowland misdeeds or inflated egos had left me jaded, Dick showed me in a more generous light.

I am very fond of this man Dorworth, who happens to be an accomplished climber, a great skier and a fine writer. It's tempting to say that excelling at those practices sculpted him into such a good man. But I see it the other way round: that being a fine human being naturally came to expression in these wild and wonderful activities. Dick once said as much of our mutual friend Steve McKinney, Dick's successor as the fastest man on skis. After mulling that over for a few years, I feel it's so fitting to reflect it back onto Dorworth.

Given the times, it was inevitable that we would meet. Climbers then, as the 1960s drew to a close, were a splinter group, hardly noticed among a sweeping American counter-cultural movement. Dick describes well that larger political and social context. He also lends a lot of local color to our life on its fringes, a small, eclectic, and fiercely nomadic band who would come to be known as dirtbags. But not yet. Nor could we conceive, in our wildest imaginations, that our scruffy lives in dusty Camp 4 in Yosemite Valley—one of the few fixed abodes that felt like home—would lead to the place being hallowed in the National Registry of Historic Places. Then, we didn't care. History was irrelevant, and Freedom (yes, Capitalize that) was the all-consuming Present (yeah, Cap that baby too).

We were both writers, too, which doubled down on the association. See, we weren't just wanderers. Nothing aimless about it. Rather, we were snobbish about a few grand places, like Tuolumne Meadows, where Dick contributed at least two of the most-repeated classic climbs, like Truckin' Drive (you'll find out why today's guidebooks have the name wrong), and retreated to a homemade redwood camper perched on an old truck, where we could catch sight of him, sitting cross-legged in the back channeling his focus into a typewriter.

Dorworth's musings on our lives and times became mainstays of a new journal, *Mountain Gazette*, the *New Yorker* of alpine life. Some of the best, like Dick's iconic piece, *Night Driving*, have anchored his earlier collections. Here, we are treated to several more.

Dorworth is dedicated to the craft of his reflections. Like the nomadic life they often depict, his stories can seem effortless, almost tossed off. They are not. Craft, probing beyond the surface of things, and attention—a pivotal goal—shine through the shapeliness of these tales. Dive on in.

A favorite story of mine in Dick's book, *The Perfect Turn*, is about climbing Mt. Shasta. Because it involves family, and Dick's family is complex. And because its crux hinges on attention, such a life-focus that it led to his, figuratively, firing his Zen master. But that's another story. Attention: one of the gatekeepers of freedom.

Here is so much more. Dick's narratives keep returning to the City of Rocks, a lovely and out-of-the-way climbing destination that erupts from backroad Idaho sagebrush. And I haven't even mentioned the tale of climbing Fitz Roy, with a star-studded cast of Fun Hogs that includes the publisher of this book. Their now-legendary 1968 climb has been the subject of at least three films and recently an entire book that includes Dorworth's setting of the context. Yet even after all that, Dick's account here ladles out fresh insight.

So much more in this volume is wonder-full. But enough. On to the pleasure of Dick's own words.

Doug Robinson
Rock Creek cabin, California

PART ONE

Climbs

CHAPTER ONE

Climbing to Freedom

IN THE SUMMER OF 1972, I was living the simple life of a normal dirtbag, disaffected, counter to the mainstream-culture, climber of the time. The mainstream of the time, exemplified by Vietnam, conspicuous consumption, and Richard Nixon, and Ronald Reagan, ran counter to the values, dreams and humanity of many but certainly not all of American climbers of the era, and the dirtbag temptations included a freeform lifestyle in which I was most comfortable. That summer I roamed around western America in a 1965 green VW camper van, with a built-in bed and some shelves for a stove and accessories, to whatever sparsely populated mountains and crags—Yosemite, Lover's Leap, Tahquitz, City of Rocks, Sawtooth, Wasatch and the Tetons—attracted the compass of the day, with sporadic detours to hot springs, folk/ rock concert gatherings and even visits with friends whose homes had foundations rather than wheels.

My marriage had exploded a few months earlier, and I inhabited an emotional/psychic wasteland in which any reminder of my wife and our year-old son caused me to want to crawl into a deep, dark hole in the earth and never come out again or climb any of the steep, bright mountains and rock faces rising out of it. There is a great deal of freedom, though not much nutrition, clear thinking or good judgment ,in such landscapes, and climbing provided a healthy balm against the bleak demons residing there. As with the physical body, happiness itself requires more nutrition than sex, drugs and rock and roll can provide, and without it the skeletal bones of thought and judgment break easily. The words of Kris Kristofferson's song "Me and Bobby McGee" resonated across the barrens:

Freedom's just another word for nothin' left to lose
Nothin' ain't worth nothin', but it's free

One completely unexpected aspect of the fallout was being contacted by an ex-girlfriend, nicknamed White Lightning. We had not communicated in years and our last attempts to do so had not been friendly, but we had a four-year-old son in common, and White Lightning suggested that they join me. Though she was not a climber, it seemed to be a possible ray of light in the darkness, but within a couple of months the same personal/ideological/social dynamics from earlier would part us again.

My road, like all roads, was less congested and freer in 1972. Destinations and down times were often determined by where and when appropriate partners were available. Early that summer, I climbed for a week with a buddy at the City of Rocks, Idaho, and never saw another climber. There were no guidebooks, so we would wander around until we saw something that looked like a route. Every now and then we would find a piton or a sling in place. There were no campgrounds, and so we set up camp wherever was convenient and close to water. Occasionally a local rancher would drive by and scowl at us, for "we" were long-haired, suspicious-looking people who spent their time crawling up the granite domes and spires that were their (the ranchers') backyard, and "they" were hard-working, honest, short-haired, reliable Mormons. There were no restaurants in the nearest town, Almo, and the one store, Tracy's, did not sell beer, so we learned to be self-contained.

Since that time the earth's population has doubled and the number of climbers in North America has grown more than that. Any modern climber who visits the City will today enjoy restaurants which sell all the alcohol money can buy (as does Tracy's), fine hot springs (Durfee), a hotel/motel, and more than 100 designated campsites that cost more for a night than we lived on for a week. Climbing is now a part of the mainstream from which we fled, and through writing, guiding and my part in the Fun Hog expedition and film, I am as guilty as any of helping make it so. I still climb as often as possible at the City, but now I find freedom in the microcosm, focusing on the move at hand, whether it be a nubbin on a smooth face, a just-right-sized crack or a terrifying sloping mantle, each more significant in the present moment than rebelling against demented authority or surviving the emotional wasteland.

I made my living in those days from teaching and coaching skiing, a few writing assignments, the rare construction stint, a month in Chile or Argentina coaching ski racing and the occasional guiding gig. When winter arrived, I would hunker down in a ski resort. A few years before I tried swimming in the mainstream, including a year as a graduate student with the idea of becoming a professor and a few months in a San Francisco office, but I simply didn't fit and couldn't discern the value others placed in such efforts and I scurried back home to the mountains where I belong. Such a lifestyle has never been conducive to stability, though whether the instability and its attendant pains and confusion are a consequence or a cause of the peripatetic lifestyle is an interesting puzzle to ponder, and I did and still do. The closest I've come to an answer is in the Buddhist concept of The Middle Way: to live between the extremes of self-denial and self-indulgence instead of on or over the edge of either.

Come early August, White Lightning, our son and I were camped in the van in a secret spot by the Snake River between Wilson and Jackson Hole, where the water and wind masked all but the loudest trucks on the nearby road. On a morning when the Teton air was as clear as innocence, I was enjoying my coffee and watching ducks play in the riffles when a car I recognized came down the dirt road. Chuck Pratt emerged from a VW Squareback and hobbled my way bent over like a crippled, smiling leprechaun. "I bring you great riches," he declared with his usual understated, literary directness.

Chuck had somehow slipped a disc the night before and was barely able to walk, much less climb. He had a client about to arrive in Rock Springs, about four hours south, and knew that I might be amenable to the great riches of guiding at a new destination—the Cirque of Towers in the Wind River Range. Pratt was a master of many aspects of life, including climbing and the minute details of his own often-solitary existence. More than two decades later I would work with Pratt as an Exum guide and live on Guides Hill as his neighbor. I marveled at the firewood around his cabin, each piece stacked with the precision of considered thought, looking like the work of a master stonemason. Meanwhile, the wooden clothespins on his clothesline, impregnated with linseed oil, looked like small pieces of fine woodwork. Some evenings, I would simply watch Pratt split firewood on a tree-round chopping block. He swung his ax with grace and a respect for minimalist efficiency. It always brought to mind the Zen maxim "Chop wood, carry water," pointing the practitioner toward each moment and task with complete focus on the present, free of the carried burdens of the past and the anticipated dreams of the future.

Chuck soon illuminated and organized the darkness of my vast ignorance of the Cirque: how to get there, where to camp and what climbs were likely suitable. He also informed me that the client had been referred by Doug Robinson in the Sierra, and he had no idea how well she climbed.

Would I meet her at the Rock Springs airport, in seven hours?

Yes.

Chuck had already bought most of the food, and he donated it to the cause. As would only be expected of an honors graduate of the Camp 4 Dirtbag School of Economics (and much more), Chuck's food bag contained the very latest in reasonably priced, lightweight, easy-to-cook dinners for backcountry gourmands: Nissin instant noodles, later popularized as ramen. I had never seen them before, but Chuck was always full of interesting surprises, and I ate ramen likely more than was good for me over the next thirty years.

We met Elizabeth that evening. This trim, dark-haired, well-groomed woman in her mid-forties adapted immediately and graciously to the unexpected circumstance. If she was disappointed at having some scruffy, unknown dirtbag, accompanied by White Lightning and a four-year-old boy, replace the iconic, well-known dirtbag Chuck Pratt, she never showed it. She expressed concern about Chuck's back, and we spent the next day and a half getting our gear and ourselves into Lonesome Lake—Elizabeth, Lightning and the boy all performed this arduous task much better than anticipated. There are few places as pristine and beautiful and with such quality climbing and comfortable camping as the Cirque of Towers in 1972. The colors of the deep-green meadow grass on the trail into the turquoise Lonesome Lake have not changed in the intervening years. Neither have the spectacular shapes and presence of the Wind River Mountains, though there are far more climbers, hikers, horseback riders—and impact—today.

Elizabeth turned out to be a charming, intelligent, well-educated, happily married housewife and mother of two who lived in the Midwest. Her husband was a successful executive with a large company. Every summer, she hired local guides to climb with her in a different mountain range of America. She had done this for several years, and it made sense to me, in the same way that my less-adventurous clients who hired me for the week a year they escaped the city to ski at their favorite resort made sense. We had a fine week climbing moderate routes on the excellent granite of the Wind River Range. Elizabeth was never rattled, never complained and worked through every difficult move with a quiet, determined grace that exuded an obvious gratefulness for the moment instead of a battle with the stone. At the end of every pitch she complimented her guide and noted the fine weather, quality of rock, the spectacular views across the valley or the colorful tents by the lake. She seemed to have a better appreciation of the experience than many clients I've known.

One dark night, over a superb Nissin noodle feast, I asked Elizabeth how she had gotten into climbing. She did not immediately respond, savoring a few bites of dinner while she gazed into the campfire. Then she recounted a story that put climbing into a stark, perhaps primordial perspective, one that I'd never entertained or needed to entertain. Until then, I'd always held that one of the attractions of climbing is that, at least for the duration of the route, the physical/emotional/mental demands of the move at hand (sic) free the climber from the insecurities, conundrums, confusion and mundane and dramatic traumas of the rest of life. In that freedom is clarity and strength that persist even after the climb is finished—for an hour, a day, a year or a lifetime, depending on the person and the significance of the climb. Climbing is not for every person and no two climbers climb for the same reasons or have the same experiences or lessons, but freedom is a word or at least a concept most climbers will identify with their efforts. For me, climbing, like skiing, provides the freedom of focusing mind, body and emotion into the present moment, the only moment that exists, and is an escape from the baggage of all the past and future moments that don't exist but which certainly burden the unfocused mind, heart and body. But when I heard Elizabeth's tale, I learned more about the significance of such freedoms and the relative meanings of the very word than I'd learned in all my thirty-four years.

Her speech revealed no accent, so I was surprised to hear that Elizabeth had been born an Austrian Jew in the late 1920s. By the time she was fourteen she was an exile in France, and then one of the fortunate few to be smuggled across the Pyrenees into Spain to avoid German concentration camps. A Basque gentleman from a small village in France who was familiar with the Pyrenees guided her group of Jewish refugees through the mountains. The journey was arduous, dangerous, frightening and involved rain, snow and unprotected climbing as consequential as being captured by the Nazi patrols. In due time, Elizabeth made it from Spain to America. The details of her flight were not made clear to me, but today there is an annual *Chemin de la Liberté*, a forty-mile hike across the Pyrenees to commemorate those fortunate enough to have escaped Nazi-occupied Europe. The journalist Edward Stourton, who made the hike in 2011, wrote:

> The *Chemin de la Liberté* (in English, the Freedom Trail or Route) takes four days. It involves climbing 4,570m (15,000ft) up and 3,350m down. The weather changes as if someone has hit the fast-forward button on the seasons. We experienced dank drizzle, boiling heat, freezing mists, snow underfoot and then more heat

in quick succession. There was a point to putting myself through all this. Every time I interviewed a survivor who had done it 'for real' during World War II, I found myself brought up short by the chasm that separated my own experiences from theirs.

Elizabeth and her group had made the journey in two days and two nights, without stopping to sleep.

Some fifteen years after crossing the Pyrenees, she returned to the Basque village to thank her guide. She found the gentleman, who was astonished when Elizabeth introduced and explained herself. She was equally astonished to hear from him that by the end of WWII he had helped hundreds of refugees (not all of them Jewish) cross to Spain, and that Elizabeth was the only one who had so far returned.

After a few days of getting to know her old guide and his family and friends, and telling her story, she hired him to retrace their path of fifteen years earlier. This time, there was no need to hide from Nazis, no hurry or necessity to take risks, no fear. They had comfortable camping gear and sufficient food, and could converse freely and loudly. When the climbing got serious they used a rope. When they grew tired they rested. They took time to appreciate the scenery, listening to the sounds of streams and wind in the trees instead of for their hunters, smelling the meadows and flowers instead of their own acrid fear. When they arrived at the Spanish border, Elizabeth experienced a very different sense of freedom than on the first crossing. The first time, she had nothing left to lose except her life—that is, everything, the only thing remaining. The second time, she had a vibrant, free existence and, perhaps just as important, a hard-earned knowledge of its true, organic value. And so, every year since, she had climbed for a week or two to be reminded of what, exactly, her new life meant.

In the process, Elizabeth enhanced and expanded my own experience of climbing. It took a few years, but I eventually crossed the wasteland into the priceless cornucopia of organic life in the free world, some of it on the road, some of it by rivers and streams, much of it moving up and down mountains. She did not tell me so, but after many years of thinking of her and her story I concluded that she was able to let go of anger, fear, heartache and loss and embrace the present moment just as it is, and, more, to be consciously grateful for that moment, the move at hand. If she had not let go, she might not have made it across the Pyrenees, seek out a Basque gentleman years later to express her gratitude, or spend a week each year experiencing and being reminded of the true meaning of climbing for freedom. It took 40 years before I chose to write about her, but all those years were informed and reflected, sometimes consciously, by Elizabeth's example of not dwelling on the past, not dreaming of the future, of concentrating the mind on the present moment, the only one that exists, whether making a move on a rock wall, appreciating a mountain landscape or enjoying a noodle dinner by a campfire after a day of climbing..

So, thank you, Elizabeth.

Fitz Roy on an unusually clear day. *photo Chris Jones*

CHAPTER TWO

The Third Ascent of Fitz Roy

A LONG, STRENUOUS APPROACH. 15,000 MILES. Ventura, California to Lago Viedma, Argentina. Five men in a cramped Ford van for over three months. A good time. From there to Fitz Roy's summit took just under two months. A strenuous time.

Fitz Roy is a startling mountain to view at any angle. From the Nevada-like Argentine desert Fitz Roy dominates its satellites, including the Cerro Torre, like Joplin at her best in front of any band. That's how we saw Fitz Roy first, from a hundred miles east in the desert.

Climbing any mountain was unique to me, a novice climber, but my mates more than covered my lack of experience.

Yvon Chouinard, who helped raise climbing standards through innovation and quality in the equipment he manufacturers, technical style, and by his part in such first ascents as the North America and Muir Walls on El Capitan.

Chris Jones, the expatriate Englishman living in San Francisco, whom we met in Lima right after his successful first ascent of the Northeast Face of Yerupaja.

Doug Tompkins, who has climbed in the "Gunks," the Tetons, the Rockies and whose one climb of the year had been the formidable Salathe Wall on El Capitan.

And the incomparable Lito Tejada Flores, master of all trades, including climbing, and our photographer. For we were in that beautiful, wild land not only to climb its dominant piece of rock, but to make a movie as important to us as the climb, a movie that started in California and needed just a few more miles.

The end of the road, October 26, 1968. We could drive no closer to the objective. With Argentine military help we were at our supply base the next morning. The was the "Parque," the Fitz Roy National Park, a lone, deserted building, a shed, an amazing plastic orange igloo left by the English Cerro Torre expedition, a meadow and stream and hundreds of Patagonian sheep.

First goal: a first ascent of the 5000-foot East Buttress of Fitz Roy. But a closer examination of the problem by Chouinard, the obvious and logical leader, convinced him this was the wrong party.

On the 28th Chris, Yvon and I made a punishing walk of eleven hours to the base of the Cerro Torre, a canyon away from Fitz Roy. We went to see the possibilities. We saw. It, too, is unique. On the way back Chouinard first spoke of the French Terray-Magnone route on Fitz Roy. Tompkins held out for the East Buttress, but by that evening the French route was our goal.

It didn't show immediately but Yvon and Chris had seriously injured their knees on that eleven hour hike. What first seemed fatigue was severe strain with cartilage damage.

On the 29th, using military horses, we established base camp in the remains of the 1951-52 French camp. It took all day in a wet snow storm. Later we covered the distance in three and a half hours with loads. Before leaving we made this trip six times.

The following day Tompkins and Chouinard broke trail for nine hours in waist-deep snow up to the ice cave site at the foot of the great barrier; Jones returned to base camp; Lito talked to the military about borrowing horses again; and I plundered the remnants of the British Cerro Torre Camp. Work had begun.

By November 5th we had made three load-carrying round trips between the green tree-filled, river-running base camp country and the stark, rock-snow clarity of ice-cave land...an hour up a steep hill to snow line, across the frozen Los Tres Lake and up the Rio Blanco Glacier to the Luncheon Rock in another hour and a half, eat, drink and rest, and another hour to two hours up more glacier and the steep snow dome to the Great Barrier and the ice cave. We were installed in a cave, ready to assault the Italian Col, following the first ascent program of Terray and Magnone as reported by M.A. Azema in *The Conquest of Fitz Roy*.

An ice cave on Fitz Roy is infinitely superior to its alternatives. The strongest tent would be blown apart by the wind, and spending several nights out in the weather there lies in the realm of the possible where imagination stumbles.

The 6th we ferried loads to the top of the Piedras Blancas Glacier where the French in 1952 had a camp, hanging them at the beginning of the first pitch. Storming the 7th. We ferried loads, improved and sealed the cave, and retreated. Yvon and Chris had knee trouble. Doug walked into his fourth crevasse of the week.

Rain next day. We moved to the French camp of 1968 (an unsuccessful East Buttress attempt). This camp, discovered accidentally while exploring the woods, came with an ingenious oven, a roofless log house, and a stream close by. A boost to our stormed-out spirits and tired bodies. None regretted the opportunity to rest. We hid in our shelter from the ever present wind and rain. Occasionally Fitz Roy was visible, snow blowing a thousand feet up from its summit. Waiting. Encore raid on the Cerro Torre camp. Early rising mornings for a color and light show unlike anything seen before. Patagonian sun-up, the Fitz Roy a red-orange monolith dominating all. By this time we read weather signs pretty well. We hadn't learned about snow clouds peeling off the Italian Col, but we knew why it was said: "Red sky at night, Sailor's delight; Red sky in morn', Sailors forlorn."

We read, wrote, bouldered, talked, walked, huddled in the shelter waiting for the rain to stop, and we made another supply trip to the Parque.

In this time I reviewed my thoughts and ideas, inventoried by actions and situations. My climbing experience (mostly in Yosemite) involved direct action: one got up in the morning, attacked the crags, did what one could and failed at one couldn't, and returned to Camp 4 with crystal clear vision of where one was at, in terms of climbing. This was different. The game was one of patience. To wait without losing cool, to keep in shape without losing reserves, to maintain will without becoming an idiot, to avoid lethargy. I was the least experienced and skilled at the game, and I relied heavily on my mates. Sometime later I understood why conversations invariably drifted from abstractions to foods we didn't have, distant places, past and future times, people who weren't there, and the superb movie we were making. The patience game is devious and sustained. A friendship with Doug and an ability on skis (for the movie) had started me on this journey to Fitz Roy. But what did I seek? Why the introspection? My notes of November 8 pose a question....

"Dorworth is alive and well in Argentina. He is happy and likes it where he is, but sometimes the awareness of his great ignorance gets him down. He doesn't even know why he eats certain foods or which foods give him the most energy or why. And in his present reading (Frazer's The Golden Bough*) he discovers that a belief in magic may have formed much of what has come to be his mind. And he wants enlightenment, the answer, the way; and he doesn't even know what these things are. How can you find something if you don't know what it is you're looking for?"*

Is climbing the answer? The way? The means? An interesting diversion? Or the individual equivalent of racing to the moon?

On the 15th Doug and I were caught in the Parque by good weather. We returned to base camp. Yvon invited us to hike to the first cave. Chris and Lito were waiting with dinner. A long day.

So was the next. Fifteen hours. Breaking trail up the Piedras Blancas was extreme labor. The fixed pins had pulled and supplies were buried, but each played his part. Yvon led the first pitch, a perfect nail up to the right of the bergschrund and he and Doug fixed five ropes in snow, ice and rock. Jones and I dug out the supplies. A perfect day, and Lito filmed until the sun went down. Then we ferried supplies up the fixed ropes and returned to the cave. Yvon could barely walk, and Chris was lame in one leg.

Yvon was unable to work on the 17th. The rest of us put in a 17 hour day. With Tompkins leading, we fixed ropes to the Italian Col, dug a tiny ice cave, ferried all the supplies to the cave, and got back to the first cave at 10 p.m. I was so tired I hallucinated while looking at the stars, connecting visually with them and seeing order in their explosive patterns in the night. Chouinard, whose climbing abilities are dwarfed by his chef talents, did not let us down that night.

The 18th was a turning point. We all went to the Italian Col, bringing up the fixed ropes, prepared to stay until the issue was decided. Lito, Chris and I worked on a new cave one hundred yards west of the Col, in the bergschrund of a glacier overlooking the Torre canyon. Doug and Yvon went to work on the French route, the first pitch recognizable by the *coins de bois*, the wooden wedges left by Terray and Magnone seventeen years before.

We had worked half an hour when Yvon showed up looking for the medical kit and Lito the medical man. While enthusiastically chopping steps in the ice below the first pitch, he had hit himself just beside the knee cap with his ice axe. A bad gash pumped blood furiously.

There we were a third of the way up Fitz Roy with a half cave, Yvon unable to move and Jones having trouble, the afternoon wearing on. We scrambled to work on the cave.

While we were about it Doug and Lito had a look around. Azema describes a black ice gully west of the Italian Col. Terray vetoed crossing the gully, though climbing appeared promising. But they were there in January, early summer, and we in November, the heart of spring; and the black ice gully was a field of snow. Azema felt a route existed on the southwest face, across the ice, beginning in the col between Fitz Roy and the Aguja de la Silla. Doug and Lito wandered over there, climbed a few pitches, and returned full of zeal. Azema was a genius.

First night in our second cave. Yvon in much pain, all of us cramped, and snow blowing in through holes in the roof. Each man had two ensolite pads, a down parka and sleeping bag. Snow covered our boots and some of our down gear. Nothing dries in ice caves and we soon acquired the habit of sleeping with boots in the foot of our bags, and socks wrapped around our upper bodies.

A Patagonian storm arrived that night. Cold, windy and brutal. Weather men could not survive in. For three days we did not go outside except for semi-daily defecation.

We were outside a few hours on the 23rd, drying gear in the wind and walking around. Sitting in the cave had depleted our conditioning, but Yvon was healing quickly. The weather returned, and we to the cave. We read the few books available. Endless talk of food. We compiled a gastronomic guide to the world of our combined experience. We ventured out to film storm scenes; the wind knocked Yvon and me down, and Lito and I froze our hands in half an hour. But we got some magnificent film. We celebrated Thanksgiving. We played word and guessing games. We spoke of existentialism and other philosophies, including our own. We got to know each other. We shared the pattern of life like a group of prisoners planning to escape and hit the city bank on the way out of town.

The wind increased. It sounded like an endless train right outside the bedroom window. In the back of our minds (or is it the collective mind?) was

The author digs out of the second ice cave to take a look.   *photo Chris Jones*

the lurking fear that the next car would jump the tracks, come through the wall, leave us naked and exposed.

We took turns at the 4 a.m. weather check. Always the same grey sky and snow falling down, up and sideways in crazy patterns and at high speed. We waited.

On December 2nd supplies ran out. We chose retreat in the storm. A classic. Wind. Cold. Snow. Iced ropes. Six rappels. Hip-deep fresh snow on the glacier. But we made it to the first cave in four hours. After an uncomfortable night we continued to base camp. I fell into two crevasses while breaking trail, and the route across Los Tres Lake was split by open water. Summer was creeping in. Our new route around the lake took an extra hour.

Doug and Lito went out (out: sixty miles to the one general store of the area) to buy supplies. Twenty days' worth. When that ran out we voted to buy more. We would out-patience Patagonian weather. We were going to get that mountain. But my enthusiasm was running low, my mind wandering to problems and places I could not see or touch, and I was functioning on duty and old-fashioned loyalty.

One day while hiking we saw two condors. "Those birds have real freedom," Yvon said, watching them control flight with giant, seldom moving wings. I remarked that they had their wings and man his mind. And when I thought about it later it seemed that what air currents were to the condor the mountain was to us. A matter of control. When I understood that I felt better, committed rather than dutified, though the same problems were still manifested.

Doug and Lito returned. A thief had raided the Parque and left everything except all our money. Money was not our concern right then, but how foolish to leave all our money down there.

Dominating all was Fitz Roy. After 15,000 miles and several months it was a few thousand feet and a couple of days above us.

The weather worsened...

...but finally cleared. This time Chris, Yvon and Doug were surprised at the Parque. The 13th Lito and I had a hard day breaking trail to the first cave. The others arrived that night. We said *le grand beau* had arrived.

We reached the second cave the next day, after ten hours of climbing and digging out fixed ropes. Tompkins and I were both bruised by falling rocks. All boots drenched. Weather perfect.

Up at 3 a.m. on the 15th. Systems tired and slow. We crossed the snowfield on the hanging glacier to the Col of the Aguja de la Silla and one pitch up the route. A morning of color—yellow reflecting rivers in the east and yellow-orange-red-white-blue sunrise, and purple western sky. Looking out across the Continental Ice Cap confirmed what we knew about morning colors. Storm. Doug and Yvon explored the route. Chris, Lito and I returned to the cave.

Doug and Yvon returned several hours later exuding an enthusiasm that soon filled us all. Wonderful to be where we were with such fine mates. The route was there, it seemed, and we would wait.

Waiting defines the boundaries of the patience game. More than anything we wanted Fitz Roy for Christmas. We were sure of victory once we got ahold of the problem, but it was an elusive bitch.

On the 19th Chouinard drew 3 a.m. door check. Light snow, no wind, breaks in the clouds. Yvon, an experienced fox, recommended the summit. He was voted down. This meant a return to the first cave. Once again we were out of food. Half way down Yvon's wisdom was apparent. A perfect day, too rare to waste ferrying supplies. We returned with ten days food. Had we blown our chance?

Without our knowledge Tompkins set the alarm ahead an hour, and we were up at 1 a.m. and moving by 2:30 a.m. of the longest day of the year in the southern hemisphere. We crossed the snowfield in darkness and were climbing with first light. A beautiful sun-up, not red in the dangerous way; incredible colors and shapes in the dawn. It was unbelievable—after thirty days in ice caves and nearly two months of work we were finally moving for the summit. The game became simple and clear, tangible, No more boundaries, just the mountain and ourselves. The weather had tested our patience and our patience had fortified our resolve.

Yvon and Doug exchanged leads, tying off ropes for the rest of us. Lito followed, more or less independent, free to film. Chris and I came last, keeping the leaders supplied with ropes. In several places everyone moved together, fourth class. After thirteen pitches of excellent climbing (and strenuous jumaring) we reached the rim of the Super Couloir. It was four in the afternoon and most discouraging.

The Fitz loomed above, the summit snowfields near and clear, but the goal was across the Super Couloir. Above, to the east, were ice-coated overhangs. Out of the question to descend into the couloir and climb out the other side. Clouds rolled by like sea mist, covering all, then passing, leaving blue sky and sun and wild mountain scenery—airplane views of some of the earth's most stark, inhospitable land. The huge snowfields of the Continental Ice Cap and Cerro Torre stole the show.

A brief rest and a few bleak moments. Tompkins rappelled into a ledge system on the south wall of the couloir. It was five in the afternoon. We were grateful for twenty hours of daylight in that part of the world in that time of year. Doug made a brilliant lead, moving up the couloir in an ice chimney and on a hoar frost-covered face. On this pitch we found a rappel sling and wedge left by our friend José Luis Fonrouge (at that moment making a new route on the Poincenot, though we didn't know it) while descending from his second ascent of Fitz Roy. Good to find the trace of a friend at that particular point.

After that came a section of fourth and easy fifth class, and then Yvon led the seventeenth pitch, a very difficult overhanging crack plastered with wind-hardened hoar frost. A hard traverse moving east, a rappel, and a short jam crack, the eighteenth and final pitch, brought us to the upper snow slopes of Fitz Roy. All that remained was a forty-five minute hike up broken rock and snow to the summit.

8 p.m., December 20, 1968. The summit of Fitz Roy. We stashed a container of photos and notes in a cairn at the summit. It is an inhospitable place, and we left after fifteen minutes of frantic film making.

Descending was another story. We moved until 2:30 a.m., making some scary rappels into unknown territory. It was dark, windy, sometimes snowing and very cold. We had been moving hard for twenty-four hours, and our instincts were dulled, our minds no longer able to control our actions with precision. Accordingly, we bivouacked on a ledge until daylight, 5 a.m., huddling together, shivering, wiggling toes and dozing.

With light we continued. By this time our ability to work smoothly and together had deteriorated immensely, and we arrived at the second cave at 10.

The next twenty-four hours were spent drinking tea, lemon jello and ovolmaltine, eating everything in sight, and sleeping. Doug, Yvon and I suffered superficial frostbite, and we kept waking up with no sensation in hands and feet.

Brisk rubbing. Sensation. Sleep.

We continued down to the first ice cave on the 22nd, and from there to the Parque on Christmas Eve. Christmas Day we got back to our car and began the journey home.

We came to Fitz Roy, made the third ascent by a new route, we all got to the summit, and we finished our movie. We accomplished what we wanted.

Words are incomplete mediums of communication, much as we love them. There is no way to know how it was except to have been there, and the experience lasts in it fullness only as long as the experience. Afterwards, something remains besides the memory, but it is something other than the experience. It is like food for the spirit—it nourishes, giving strength for another day.

Just below the summit, when we knew it was in the bag, Chouinard summed it up, "Well, now we have earned our freedom for a while."

Wally Rothgeb outside our igloo on the Kahiltna Glacier, Mount McKinley
author's photo

CHAPTER THREE

A Hell of a Climb

Education by Fire on McKinley (1970)

Nobody climbs mountains for scientific reasons. Science is used to raise money for the expeditions, but you really climb for the hell of it.
—Edmund Hillary

If you are going through hell, keep going.
—Winston Churchill

I WOKE FROM THE DEEP SLEEP that follows an overworked day. The grey Alaska May night seeped into the igloo covering its contents with opaqueness. My heart crashed in my chest like an out-   of-control pile driver—hard, fast and unnatural. I sat up, struggling with my mummy bag zipper in a claustrophobic frenzy. The first function of my body was unexpectedly berserk and I was only breathing fear. Instinctively, I forced myself to take in air. Hard. Then I forced it out. Again. Pull in. Push out. My lungs weren't working automatically, the way they always had, and my heart beat too hard, too fast. The life forces were out of control or—more accurately perceived with the gift of contemplation not available to one whose heart and lungs have suddenly changed from angels of life to devils of fear—the life forces were showing me that the illusion of control was just another self-serving habit if not addiction. "O shit," I thought, "I'm dying. O shit." My mind went to sunny, comfortable California and the fine, controlled life I had there where everything you need is just around the corner for the asking, but in the present reality at

10,000 feet on Mt. McKinley I couldn't breathe. I pulled in air. Pushed it out. O shit. Pull in. Push out. Shit. My heart was flopping around with the rhythm of an angry tuna in the bottom of the boat. I concentrated on slowing it down but it's hard to focus when you're drowning.

Air is precious.

In a short time measured by interminable mind journeys and heart beats my lungs began doing their own thing, and my tuna fish chest became a regular, strong rhythm.

What the fuck was that?

I looked around in the dim light to make sure the physical world and my place within it were the way I expected. Wally was next to me breathing softly, asleep. The igloo entrance let in a diffused light from a clear night that never reached complete darkness on McKinley in mid-May. Familiar world. The security and illusion of control. I could see Wally which meant the others were surely in the igloo. Relief for the mind but the body was working harder than the efforts of sleep demanded. I listened to my heart and lungs gradually slow down to a gentle, regular rhythm and considered waking Doctor Lito, but cold conquered fear and I zipped up my bag and rested my head on a pillow of rope and wool knickers to wait for warmth. I stumbled into sleep trying to determine what had just happened to my body, somehow already returning to the illusory comfort of control.

In the morning I felt fine and dismissed the episode as an aberration and didn't mention it to my mates. Our fourth and thus far hardest day on the mountain stretched out before us like Sisyphus' rock. We were moving fast and what reason could there be to pause when we were moving so well? Six days earlier I had been at sea level in London, England and had gone from there to Anchorage to Talkeetna to 7000 feet on the Kahiltna Glacier where I had carried heavy loads to 10,000 just above Kahiltna Pass. We had moved fast, helped on the night of the third day with the discovery of the well-made two-room igloo left by a party that couldn't be far ahead. North-westerners, we decided, and highly organized.

Moving fast and pushing hard, speed and extension, have a catch:

the faster you go and the harder you push the faster you want to go and the more you expect from yourself. Catch 22 of climbing. It catches different climbers in various ways at odd times in traps both subtle and profane, but every man has a limit. Our first three days on the West Buttress of Mt. McKinley were marked by speed and effort, but in the heated moment of putting one foot in front of the other hour after hour it sometimes seemed interminably slow, laboriously dull and at the same time the most beautiful, fulfilling movement a body could make. We told ourselves we were on our way toward the first ski descent from the summit of Mt. McKinley, and for some strange reason(s) were confident that we would do it. First we had to reach the summit using skis for the climb as well as the descent. For some strange reason(s) we viewed ourselves as a strong, well-balanced party of six to play the expedition game together on a peak higher than any of us had been before. Though we had all (except one) managed to get up some respectable climbs in the past, none of us had been to 20,000 feet before and some people are particularly unsuited to the rigors of breathing low-oxygen-content air. I am one. Like many things of life seen in retrospect it is unbelievable (and really irresponsible) that I had never heard of Acute Mountain Sickness (AMS), High Altitude Pulmonary Edema (HAPE) or High Altitude Cerebral Edema (HACE), but I had not. One medical description reads:

> *Severe AMS can also take the form of High Altitude Pulmonary Edema (HAPE.) This is where excess fluid develops in the lungs, either in the lung tissue itself or in the space normally used for gas exchange. This means individuals are unable to perform gas exchange properly, and so person cannot get enough oxygen to function normally. It is caused, again, by poor acclimatization and is often more common in males, although it is not clear whether this is behavior related or due to genetic susceptibility. HAPE can occur without the traditional signs of AMS. Indications of HAPE include:*
> *Difficulty walking or inability to keep up*
> *A tight-feeling chest*
> *Congestion*

A chesty cough, possibly accompanied first by a clear phlegm and later by blood.
Extreme fatigue/weakness
Gurgling sound whilst breathing. If you place an ear to the victim's chest, you may hear crackling or gurgling noises.
Poor judgment
Breathlessness during rest
Rapid heart rate (90 to 100 bpm at rest)

Personally, I think that poor acclimatization caused by moving too high too fast is behavior related, though genetics, specifically gender genetics, may play a role.

Like most climbing expeditions, ours was composed of diverse individuals whose strengths and differences we hoped would compliment and support (and cover) each other. For the most part our expectations were met.

Doug Tompkins, 27: expedition organizer and planner, a dark haired athletic man of medium build, a radiant smile when happy and a black seriousness when not, Doug remembered another time we had spent a couple of months in soaked leather boots and frozen feet walking and climbing on glaciers, and he had gotten the best overboots ever made for us. We also had good packs, new touring bindings and skis, sleeping bags, gloves and everything we needed. Tompkins is good to his friends.

Lito Tejada-Flores, 27: all around savant, he was first to raise the proposal that since we were going to McKinley and were all accomplished skiers, why didn't we just ski it? Why not? Film maker, writer, skier, climber, ski instructor, linguist, punster and friend, Lito is a man for all seasons in all ways. He had already published the iconic essay "Games Climbers Play," required reading which begins with this quote from Louis Arragon, "Reality is the apparent absence of contradiction." An ex-military medic, Lito was, fortunately for me, expedition doctor.

Juris Krisjansons, 34: a gentle Latvian 6'1" 180 pounds of muscle bear with soft blue eyes, wide shoulders and a calm demeanor. At the end of World War II Juris and his parents fled Latvia. When they arrived in America Juris was 12 and spoke Latvian and German and no English. Though he earned a degree in aeronautical engineering from Ohio State University he made a career of doing whatever it took to climb up and ski down mountains. At the time that included being in charge of keeping avalanches and skiers separated in Jackson Hole, Wyoming. Easily the physically strongest in the group, Juris came straight from Yosemite to Alaska with a determination to match his strength.

Rick Sylvester, 28: the physically smallest among us, fresh off the Haute Route from Chamonix to Zermatt on skis, the most experienced in ski touring, in superb physical shape and with an impressive climbing and skiing resumé. We all anticipated that Rick would be a valuable addition and companion on the expedition. Lito and I had met Rick in a lift line at Squaw Valley two years earlier when Lito saw a familiar hat on an unfamiliar head and asked its wearer where he had gotten it. Lito had lost that hat while skiing in Leysin, Switzerland in 1965 and Rick had found the hat in the snow a year later and was wearing it.

Wally Rothgeb, 23: ski racer, adventurous spirit, friend and, most important, good man. He had almost no climbing experience but was an excellent skier. Wally, nearing the end of a fine racing career with the U.S. Ski Team and with just a few credits left before graduating from college, was at a transition point in life and looking for new horizons. A week earlier he had dropped by Tompkins' home in San Francisco just to say hello. He found Doug preparing for Alaska to climb and ski off the highest peak in North America. Would Wally like to come? Sure, why not?

And me, Dick Dorworth, 31: I had spent the winter working on a ski film and skiing in Switzerland and France. I was enthused and positive about our objective on McKinley and our collective abilities to accomplish it. I was about to receive a hell of a rigorous education about the depths of my own ignorance and some physical limits of my own body which it (and I) had never before encountered.

That fourth day was as hard as the scenery through which we moved was resplendent. We carried eight days of supplies. In the cramped quarters of the igloo everyone cannot get ready at the same time and

I was the first out. Lito helped me get my pack on and remarked on its heaviness. Good for the ego and will. Makes you grateful for people like Lito and that you are carrying your weight in life. An hour later I was reminded of how heavy life can be even when lightened by perfect weather, mountains, snow, ice fall wild scenery, clean air, good companions and the present experience of putting an idea into action—climbing McKinley and skiing back down. With the advantages of a two foot wide snowshoe track left by the igloo constructors, tight fitting seal skins on the bottoms of our skis and the relief of being off the slow rising Kahiltna Glacier and onto the steeper actual mountain it was as easy as possible. One foot attached to ski moves ahead and the seal skin prevents the ski from moving back, and the other foot moves ahead, over and over and over. Heavy pack. Heavier with every step. Up a winding path through crevasses and ice falls, around house size blocks of ice in a rainbow world hidden in white, Doug and I roped together and the others scattered behind.

At just over 11,000 we encountered the six igloo makers from Washington. They were pleasant fellows going down for supplies, happy to have us use their igloo and just as surprised that we were moving so fast. They said so and reported they had been on the mountain for two weeks. Even though I'd never heard the terms acclimate, acclimatize or acclimatization something like a shooting star crossed the dense depths of my mind, but I pushed it aside and pushed on. They continued down. A little later Juris passed us and by noon Juris, Doug and I were resting at the Washingtonian's 12,500 foot camp. I felt strong and put aside any thought of the strange wake-up call of the night before as an unexplainable fluke.

Sylvester caught up to us. Wally and Lito were far behind. Rick's physical strengths exceed his social skills and it was a poor time for him to come on strong with his opinion that Doug and I were not carrying our share of the load. It was not his opinion, he emphasized, but Lito's, and Lito was a couple of hours behind. Rick's short diatribe was demoralizing and surprising and its assertion wasn't true and we all knew it. More, Lito had said just the opposite the last time I'd seen him a few hours before, but shirking your share in an expedition is a cop-out and hearing an expedition mate accusing you of coping out is demoralizing. Lito, Doug and I had played this game before and I couldn't understand Lito saying such a thing, but he wasn't there and so Doug and I picked up our somehow heavier packs and headed for Windy Corner.

The Washington crew had told us we would have to use crampons for this stretch, and they were nearly right. Juris took off his skins and side-stepped. Doug and I barely made it with skins, climbing more on arms than feet. I had one scare when a skin came off my ski but the thought of a thousand foot fall spurred me on. By the time I reached Windy Corner my arms felt like I'd climbed up there on my hands. Rick, the most experienced at high mountain touring, was equipped with nifty ski crampons none of the rest of us had seen before. Next time the rest of us would know about this handy tool.

We rested and ate at Windy corner, 13,300 feet. Above us the route took a circuitous route through a crevasse field well-marked by flags put there by Ray "Pirate" Genet, McKinley's first guide whom we had visited in Anchorage. We discussed the situation and decided to rope up, don crampons, leave some food for Wally and Lito and continue on to the site of our next camp at 14,200 feet. Doug and Juris roped up and were first to leave. I was occupied with the details of leaving a food cache, arranging my pack and putting on crampons when I noticed that Rick was no longer with me. He had left without a word, though I had assumed after the discussion that he and I would rope up together. But—there he was, a hundred yards up the route, alone, on skis, moving on. "Well," I thought, "... ?????"

Half an hour later I caught up to him sitting amidst a grand design of crevasses and ice blocks exchanging skis for crampons. I asked him what he was doing, and he replied that in case I didn't have eyes to see he was taking off his skis and putting on his crampons, and I shouldn't wait for him. I didn't. Soon I caught up with Juris and Doug who wondered why I was walking around unroped in a crevasse field. I didn't know but I certainly felt more secure after tying in with them.

By the time we reached the camp site we were fatigued enough to relish some relaxation and Doug was suffering with a severe headache. Lito and Wally were tired, lagging behind with heavy packs, so we determined that Doug should stay and set up camp and Juris and I would go down and help Lito and Wally with their loads. Rick wandered in and, while he felt and said he had carried his share for the day (which was true), he had left his skis below and had to return for them. Juris and I roped up and offered our individualist expedition mate a place on the rope, but he felt ropes an unnecessary encumbrance and carried on alone and unroped.

Even going back down was hard. For the second time that day we passed the boys from Washington, coming back up with loads. We reached Wally and Lito at Windy Corner. They were both tired but continuing to put one foot in front of the other. An immediate and short conversation with Lito and Rick clarified that Rick had misunderstood both the meaning and intention of Lito's words about our loads in the morning. We aired the matter and started back up with Juris and Lito on one rope, Wally and I on another. Rick insisted on soloing the crevasse field alone, unroped. Half way to camp he stepped into a sidehill crevasse and in the process of throwing himself sideways in order to avoid falling into the hole he dropped his ski pole which slid down the trough of the uncovered crevasse. Fortunately, Juris and Lito were close by and they gave Rick a retrieving belay. Eventually, despite ourselves, the rigors of the seemingly ever growing mountain and the diminishing oxygen levels of its increasingly secretive air we made it to camp.

Lito was unlucky enough to wind up nearest food and stove in the four man tent, and he spent hours preparing brews and food while the rest of us collapsed. Doug had bad headaches and my breathing process was like an automobile engine that periodically sputtered for no discernible reason and then resumed running normally. I couldn't detect the exact malfunction but I knew the internal motor was not ok. That evening we discussed our strategy and voted to devote the next day to rest. For Wally, Doug, Lito and me there was no question—we needed it. Juris felt he could continue without it but thought the acclimatization and rest would be beneficial. Sylvester was dead against a day of rest which he insisted he didn't need, and his disgust with our fatigue and weakness was both plain and plainly spoken. Rick had worked on the ski film I was involved with the previous winter in Switzerland and had been included on the expedition at my instigation. I thought his physical strength would be a great asset to our endeavor and he pressed me to let him join us. I had spoken to Tompkins who barely knew Rick and he agreed that his strength would make us a stronger party. Rick was included at the expense of another friend whom we knew better but who was a weaker climber.

That was a hard night for my breathing. I coughed and felt the wretchedness of every mammal that can't get enough oxygen and I don't think I slept at all, though you never really know when it's like that. Strong pains in my chest, coughing, heavy heart beat. Breath is the control mechanism of life and when it's out of control there's not much to say, but how easy to think of the next day and rest.

And a good day it was. Fine weather. Hot. Too hot for six in a one door four man tent at 14,200 on McKinley. A day doing nothing. Bliss, no matter what the temperature. My health didn't improve the way I'd hoped, but it didn't deteriorate and I was optimistic and even thinking about the reality of our endeavor with a bit more clarity. During the day I began something that should have been considered in more careful detail much earlier: looking at some of Bradford Washburn's aerial photographs alongside a topographic map of McKinley. After four days on the mountain I knew more about what that map and those photos represented in terms of climbing up and skiing down, and my perspective had changed. As the most experienced skier in the group, I suggested and by a 5 to 1 vote it was agreed that we would carefully check three different slopes above us before deciding to carry our skis up them. With six skiers the odds might be higher than the risk warranted, and a fall would be a long one. If we had had warm, stiff Lange boots, if it were at half the altitude, if we had ridden to the top in a gondola, if there were one instead of six of us it could be a different story. However, it was an old story and, among other things, I, for one, was learning the first small lessons in an education that would continue about the physical limitations of my own cardio-vascular system dealing with the thin oxygen of higher elevation climbing. Altitude is a relative term, depending on the system dealing with it, and mine wasn't dealing very well and never would.

I wasn't the only one hurting that day. Wally and Doug were slightly snow blind which didn't alleviate Tompkins' headaches. Lito was worked. Rick was dragging more than he liked to let on. Juris seemed to have a source of energy not available to the rest of us, a great Latvian life force that did not wear down.

Not much sleep the night of May 20th, short as those Alaska nights are. Once I woke and was forced outside for a bitter cold urination. I was coughing, wheezing, shivering and weak, but what a universe greeted my wretched being! A full moon night covered the dusk of Alaskan May reflecting off the white-blue-ice Mt. McKinley world, and more wonder than bewilderment at the sensation of being not of this earth and time. My very transitoriness illumined the precious nature of the place, the companions, the experience and the moment that would never come again. We seek adventure in far out places to clear the mind and spirit of its camouflage. I know not how long I stood in that place of diamond clarity before shivering and numbness in my feet reminded me that time is relative even to the transitory. I returned to tent and bag and companions with incredible happiness and a desire for warmth. I slumbered until nearly 1 a.m. when I could no longer ignore with a clear conscience the preparatory activity in the tent.

We were heading for the summit with four day's supplies. By 2:30 a.m. the first rope of Doug and Juris was nearly ready. Lito and I were closest and would obviously be the second rope. (I had an ulterior motive for roping up with Lito: he was usually the slowest and I was feeling weak and unsure of my own physical capabilities.) Wally, the least experienced, was slow in getting his things together. Rick woke up long enough to be served breakfast but was fast asleep again. Doug requested that Rick get up but Rick was barely stirring when Lito and I took off. The cold hadn't warmed any and I was glad when we finally were organized and on the move at a slow pace, touring bindings clacking with each step in the morning air. Tompkins and Kristiansen were moving fast and I was impressed because just 12 hours earlier Doug had been silenced and stopped with headache, snowblindness and fatigue. I focused on Lito's pace, right pole left ski, left pole right ski, knowing that I was much faster than he at this and really looking forward to a relaxed pace behind him.

That's when I knew I was in trouble, or, rather, that's when I admitted to myself that I was in more than trouble and was a dumb (and in deep) shit. It was all I could do to keep up with the slow-paced Tejada-Flores who never hurries but always gets there. I knew immediately I wasn't going to 17,000 that day, but I didn't know how to just turn around, how to listen to the wisdom of my body, how to admit to my mates that I was coming undone. I was struggling to make each move and wondering what to do or say when we saw Doug and Juris, a few hundred yards higher, remove skis and continue on crampons. Skis work fine on snow, even steep snow, but when snow turns to ice skis must be removed, put on the packs, and crampons attached to boots. The decision had been made and we knew it was the correct one.

Through the clear, sound-carrying air came Sylvester's voice announcing to Wally and world that he was going to take his skis to the summit. Otherwise, why make the climb?

I felt too miserable in body to think about it just then, but I remember wondering if in some other sphere of his humanity Sylvester didn't feel just as bad. I couldn't dwell on it as my own problems were mounting with each step, and by the time Lito and I reached the others' skis I was shaking with cold and weakness and breathing with lungs that couldn't be satisfied. The simple task of removing skis and donning crampons loomed monumental in my mind. I stood pondering the inevitable when we suddenly noticed Juris and Doug just above us and coming down. Doug was completely wiped and could go no further that day.

I hope never again to be so grateful for another man's misfortune and inability to continue.

New Plan

Doug and I would return to 14,200 for a day of rest and acclimatization. Lito and Wally would return to 10,800, spend the night, and return to 14,200 with more supplies. Rick and Juris would ferry loads to 17,000 and return to Camp 4.

Doug and I immediately roped up and returned to the tent. As we left Rick was insisting he would take his skis up, regardless of what Juris chose to do. A suspicion rocketed by but my own problems were as immediate and strong as my body was not, and, besides, who would ever think such a thing?

At the camp we left our skis and packs just lying in the snow and crawled into our bags, removing only boots. Doug's feet were an ivory hue, so we worked on those for 20 minutes before settling into down bags and our miserable selves. The morning's exertions had broken an entire inner level of my ability to cope with my rapidly deteriorating health. When Doctor Lito arrived I told him something was beyond control and that I felt really bad. Poor Lito. He became pensive and unusually silent. Lito likes to talk and is a great conversationalist but when he acts he knows why and where and wastes no time in idle chatter. He scurried over to the nearby Washingtonians' camp and borrowed a stethoscope and came back and listened to the gurgling in my chest, consulted with neophyte climber Doctor Rothgeb, asked and was answered how I felt, and made a decision: pulmonary edema. Many years later Wally commented, "I will never forget the sound of Dick's lungs gurgling through the stethoscope at Windy Pass. Once you hear that sound, you have a new appreciation of the dangers of pulmonary edema."

Only possible treatment: diuretics and retreat to lower elevation. Immediately.

But time rushes and crawls to its own tempo and Juris and Rick were back from 17,000 by the time Lito and I were ready to leave. Juris wanted a third on the rope the next time he climbed with Sylvester. No further explanations were needed but I was too sick to care. Thirty-five yellow snow holes and three and a half hours later Lito had coaxed me down with continual chatter, good cheer, acute intelligence and sympathy for my fatigue without allowing stops (except to pee) until we reached the igloo. Lito is a man for all seasons.

We crawled into the igloo and I slept for five hours, woke up long enough to consume a Lito cuisine and fell immediately to sleep for thirteen hours. By the morning of the 22nd my body was back in control of its functions, though weak, but I had been given a lesson in how humans make habit of the precious, tenuous gift of life and call it control. The depth of my dreams, the simplicity of my thoughts and the clarity of my feelings about those thoughts was part of the lesson that life is a gift.

That afternoon we were surprised by a visit from Juris, Wally and Doug. They were concerned about me and about what Lito might do if my condition required more than lower altitude, and they decided to check on me and to get more supplies. I was weak but getting better by the hour and it was agreed that the next day we would all go back up, everyone but me carrying a load. Rick had refused to come down. He told them he felt too tired from the trip to 17,200 to carry another load up from the igloo. Fair enough, for he had worked harder than any of us except Juris, but we were concerned about Sylvester in terms of the expedition as well as in terms of himself. We discussed it but came to no conclusion, for who can answer another man's problem?

That night we ate and talked and planned for the coming day and those following as if plans and control were synonymous. My health improved by the hour. We slept in the igloo on summit dreams.

Tompkins, as usual, was first up and engrossed in morning chores. The rest of us arranged our packs from the sitting sleeping bag position and waited for Doug to serve the much anticipated morning meal. Half way through cooking breakfast Tompkins was leveled by a sudden headache and sickness that would crack his skull and rot his strength. He returned to his sleeping bag and Juris resumed cooking. When the meal was eaten and everyone ready to start the day Doug was unable to move.

New plan. I would stay in the igloo with Doug. If he got worse I would get him down to the landing field and radio for a plane. The others would go up to 14,200, wait one day for us in case Doug was better and then proceed to the summit without us. They left me in the igloo with the sound of Doug's heavy breathing and the suspicion that this hell of a climb was not going to be ours.

An hour later began one of those episodes of life that afterwards seems hard to believe really happened.... Sylvester showed up. I was surprised but Doug was asleep and it was nice to have someone to talk with, until Rick announced that he was abandoning the expedition. Oh no! A bummer in the works! I spent the better part of the next hour trying to convince Rick that the expedition was a unity and too small to lose a climber of his strength and caliber. No one wanted him to leave. We would all feel a sense of failure if he went. He would regret it the rest of his climbing life. He had asked to be included on this trip and wasn't being a very good friend by leaving it early, and this was an expedition of friends as much as climbers. Besides, where did he think we were? On the Apron in Yosemite where if it isn't going just right you can rappel off and stroll back to Camp 4 where there is every chance of better company? Rick accepted lunch and my unwanted support and advice in silence and mysterious shivers which sometimes shook his body. I was on the other side of the igloo preparing hot tea and delivering my monologue of saving Sylvester from bumming us out, when he did just that.

Rick told me to save my breath because as soon as the others had left the tent the previous day he had soloed to the summit of McKinley. He didn't ski down and had just gotten back, having bagged his summit, and only stopped by to pick up his book (appropriately enough "The Magus" by John Fowles) and a few other things. I suppose the only reason he told me about his climb was so that I would shut up.

I did. There was nothing to say that would have been very good. I just turned away to look at the natural mountain scenery and get it back in control. Ho ho. It is beautiful atop the Kahiltna Glacier across from Kahiltna Pass. Over the pass to the northwest you can see green Alaska wildlands whose future has already been sold to the highest bidding oil company. I thought about nature and ecology and mankind for some reason, and it came to me that the difference between competition and cooperation is consideration. I wondered what Rick really thought about us—Doug, Lito, Wally, Juris and me—and what he felt and thought about himself. I was really angry, but Rick had sort of soloed McKinley with his expedition mates acting as unknowing support crew which, of course, tarnishes if not removes the solo label, a good feat by a strong mountaineer that no one can ever take away from him. He had covered the whole route unroped and obviously had some luck. Combining friendship and climbing brings out the best in each, but I'd rather have a friend than a feat. Not everyone feels that way and neither did I in other times, but there wasn't much to say when Rick came out of the igloo with his things and said he was going on down to the landing field, catch a plane and leave.

Rick left and I went in and made lunch for Doug and woke him up and told him what Rick had done. It was better for everyone that Doug was asleep while Rick was there. I was angry and disappointed with Rick, but Doug, a scrapper at heart, was offended and challenged. We spent the rest of the afternoon discussing the differences in attitudes towards what we both agreed was a failure of one member of our group. We talked about our feeling that we had all lost something more than we knew how to measure. Perhaps we climb because the mountains give us what we lack as human beings. We climb because of our immeasurable need.

We woke the morning of the 24th to find the igloo entrance filled with snow. Two feet of fresh powder had fallen in the night and a couple of thousand feet higher Windy Corner was earning its name. It was cold and we procrastinated for a couple of hours before determining that we were neither physically nor psychologically prepared to move up to 14,200 feet in 2 feet of new snow. The fun was gone and we were done with a hell of a climb.

Instead, we had the best day and most fun of the entire adventure, skiing several miles down the Kahiltna Glacier after a ragged start. Our packs were huge, somewhere around 70-80 pounds. We started skiing alpine style with our heels locked down and every time we unweighted to begin a turn the packs on our backs would move in the opposite direction of our turn and take us with it. After a few inelegant falls into the soft powder snow and strenuous efforts getting back up I remembered something I had learned as a young skier and hadn't thought of or used in many years—the Telemark turn. (Remember, this was 1970 before the Telemark renaissance in American skiing, before Park Rangers lived on McKinley to assist clueless climbers like us, before SAT phones, before the old official name of McKinley was pushed aside by years of common usage and officially renamed 'Denali' by President Obarma in 2015.) Doug had never seen a Telemark turn but he is a quick learner and we were soon floating down the Kahiltna glacier carving the best Telemark turns that slope had ever seen and having a wonderful time in the present process of retreat. Since we had elected to ski unroped in order to more fully enjoy the skiing we also had a wonderful amount of good luck. At one point I came out of a turn with too much speed to do anything but continue skiing over a ten foot wide dark blue slice in the snow that was obviously a snow bridge over a not shallow crevasse and I thanked Ullr and slowed down in that order as soon as I crossed it.

Near the base of the glacier up which we had to climb to the landing field we encountered some Japanese climbers on their way to try a new route on the West Face. They were friendly, gracious and very happy to tell us that our friend Rick was still at the landing field with the rest of their expedition. Apparently, he was unable to make the radio work and couldn't call for a flight out. This information gave Doug more energy and enthusiasm for the present moment than he'd had in a few days and as the Japanese party continued toward the West face Doug rushed on toward our camp to see what assistance he could be to Rick. I was tired and took my time, having already set a Pacifist example which Doug followed.

A comic memory that isn't all that funny: trudging up the landing field spur of the Kahiltna Glacier, afternoon sun at my back, the Northwest face of Mt. Hunter before me, dazzling snow-ice-rock walls rising up on both sides. My debilitating fatigue had broken the visual barriers so that snow white was scattered into a billion crystals of color and a palpable gratitude that my physical work for the day and the climb was nearly finished. Despite some disappointment it was a fine state of mind, a magical time in a landscape that is worth the effort to see. And echoing off the walls around was the shouting of Tompkins telling Sylvester what he thought and how he felt, speaking for all of us in his loudest voice. By the time I arrived it was silent. There was nothing left to say. Doug and Rick were sitting outside the tent, looking in opposite directions. The members of the Japanese party camped next door were pretending that we weren't there until I said hello and waved. Then they smiled and invited us over for hot drinks and snacks, which we accepted. Then Doug got the radio working and contacted Cliff Hudson, the good pilot of Talkeetna, who said he'd be right in to pick us up. We made friends with the Japanese and exchanged addresses and sold equipment and discussed the world scene and a couple of mutual friends as thoroughly as their 20-word English and our 0-word Japanese vocabulary would allow. But you don't need words to communicate if you truly want to, and when Hudson showed up an hour later I felt sad to leave our new friends. Doug and I were back in warm San Francisco within 48 hours.

Wally, the novice climber, later described what happened after they left Doug and me at the igloo: "As Yuri, Lito and I were headed back up from the igloo, we encountered Rick skiing down. He stopped and told us that he was going down to catch the plane back to Talkeetna. We asked "What about the summit?" He informed us that he had summited and was going home and then skied off. As I recall, Juris (a man of few words) had some things to say about Rick's character and ethics. We continued on to Windy Pass. We continued on to the snow/ice cave at 17,000 feet. After another night of difficult sleep for me we started for the summit. As all through the trip, we had perfect weather. Since we each had a different pace, we saw no need to rope up. We were invincible and pioneering the fast and light style.

"As I was hiking toward the summit on the broad low angle ridge on firm wind-packed snow, I looked down into a deep gully to the right, thinking that if someone slipped and slid down there it would be a very bad situation. If you were hurt at all it would have probably been fatal.

"Juris was the first to make it to the summit. I kept Lito in my sight and just put one foot in front of the other. Three steps and rest. Three steps and rest. Don't rest too long, just a couple of extra breaths. Finally the summit with Juris and Lito. No camera as Doug was the expedition photographer. After a little time on the summit we headed back down to the cave at 17,000 feet and spent the night there. The next morning we went down the fixed ropes and then skied from Windy Pass to the igloo at 10,000 feet. The mountaineers from Seattle were gone. They had left one or two of their 5 gallon metal cans filled with all sorts of delicacies, shrimp and all sorts of food that we had not carried. We gorged ourselves, spent a night well fed, slept well due to the lower altitude and had a great ski down to the landing strip the next morning. Unroped of course.

"Cliff landed the plane with beer, milk and oranges. We loaded the plane and took off down the glacier. I remember that the stall warning seemed to squawk for an awfully long time before we gained some altitude. Back in Anchorage we ended up at the house we had crashed at on the way in. Lito and I took wonderful hot showers. Juris decided that he really did not need a shower. I am sure that other passengers on the plane the next day would have disagreed with him."

Mount McKinley from the Kahiltna Glacier   *author's photo*

Doin' the Dog on Half Dome   *photo Royal Robbins*

CHAPTER FOUR

Doin' the Dog

On Half Dome with Royal Robbins in 1970

ALL CLIMBERS KNOW ROYAL ROBBINS—hard man with lots of time on Yosemite walls. Even non-climbers know about Half Dome. No need to introduce either.

Royal thinks he owns Half Dome. He's written that he wants it, and maybe he wants the entire valley. Every route on the north wall in all the photographs belongs to Robbins. There were three. One hasn't had a repeat and one has had one. Robbins territory.

Warren Harding, too, has survived the years with good reason; and in early hot July he finally bathooked his way up the South Face of Half Dome. There's a connection between Harding, Robbins and Half Dome (causing consideration of "Bathook and Robbins" as a title), but the link is lost in the mists of Yosemite big-wall mythology, which they both love. So I wondered what Robbins thought about Harding hooking up, so to speak, the backside of Royal's rock.

Don't know, but a few days after Harding finished his route I was beaching with my lady, Jane, at Tenaya Lake, soaking up sun, rest and pleasure when Robbins plops down in the sand with a proposition in mind: a new route on Half Dome.

Five seconds passed before the answer could surface. The delay had several sources. I had never done a Grade VI, except a jumared one; the dry summers plague Yosemite walls between June and September; I'd never pounded pitons with the finesse required for what is known as an A4 pin and could not conceive the delicacy of an A5er. Who knew what

45

miniscule cracks were there? Not me. I'd only climbed 10 days in a year. Would I flame out? Was I experienced enough? Ready for a major route? A new one? What if I couldn't do it? What if I died?

Comfy beach. Nice lady.

But, what the hell. Only one way to know, and there's really nothing better to do than find out. Is there? And Robbins is such fun to climb with. He is so good. Plays so hard. Besides, he's my friend and he asked. You gotta go with the times, grow with them. Time to find out about those walls. What the hell.

Twenty four hours later we were at the base of the wall after a five hour frontal approach, an interesting adventure itself. Heaps of man signs there: tin cans, glass bottles, paper, empty plastic water bottles, webbing slings and old clothes. Others had come before.

Our luck found water trickling from the wall, saving a two hour walk to the spring. I asked Royal how much water we would take. "Quartandahalfperdayperman," he said, looking as if I'd questioned the Trinity. I hoped July heat might necessitate, at least allow, more survival than the classic Yosemite formula. Not so. Not so. I held out for 10 Sportade packets, a bag of lemon drops, a water bottle of fruit cocktail and some ginseng. I didn't know, but I knew my own system.

Sustained by minimum food and water and armed with dozens of nuts, clogs and pitons, we leapt upon the northwest face of Half Dome at four in the afternoon. Royal first. He led 30 feet before aiding himself. Precious little went for free after that. The rope ran out regularly. I played diligent belayer, shouting out the remaining rope at appropriate intervals. When no extra rope between us remained, he asked if I'd move up a bit. I climbed 10 feet to a tiny foothold and watched the loose rope climb higher. I moved up again. It was a difficult place and my arms and hands were tired long before the rope pulled taut. It had begun.

I cleaned and banged up to a timely ledge. Hot and much too tired for only having climbed a long and a short pitch. Bad sign. Got to live cleaner. The incredible Valley Yosemite below. A Hobbit world of elf forms, dark Strider shadows, rich green separated from pale blue sky by orange yellow sunset giving way to night. Robbins, making his seventh ascent on the face, had never seen so few lights in the Saturday night valley. Good sign. My partner gave me his Ensolite pad to sleep upon.

The Sabbath is the day of rest, but we were honest and I set off first. Rotten. Crumbly. Unclimbable without nuts. Flaky. Dirty. Terrible. Shitty! A boulder balanced on a flake right in the way. Knock it off or throw it down? Succumbing to ego rather than chancing faith, I told the belayer to move to one side of the ledge. Then I tossed the boulder down on top of the water bottles on the other side of the ledge. Less than a quart was lost but it thinned the already skinny formula. I was aided up the rest of the pitch by some dry Robbins humor.

At the end of my rope was a terrifying belay. Royal came up, complimented my pitch, complained of my anchors, and commented that a fair amount of suffering might be ahead.

We gardened another pitch each. I felt terrible, alien and dry as the rock in a world unfit for humans. Candy and food wrappers littered every ledge and many cracks. I thought we must be on an often-climbed route, but Royal assured me it was just tourist garbage thrown from above. Hikers on top of Half Dome seem fascinated with throwing rocks, pebbles, boulders and even beer cans down the face. You hear them coming, turning over in the air, making a sound like a heavy prop gone mad. You shrink inside and scrunch against the rock. You get a hand or arm over your head and don't question what good that might do. You exhaust your obscenity repertoire. You understand something of the soldier in combat. You are outraged at people's ignorance. You are pissed.

After two more insane pitches we found ourselves inside a huge chimney on a chockstone big enough to stand two or curl one. It was my tiredest moment.

"What shall we name the route?" I asked.

"The Dog," he said. Sometime later Royal invented another Greek or Roman name which I keep forgetting. The spontaneity of the first christening somehow sticks in mind, and The Dog it is to me.

It was my turn, but darkness was near so the faster Robbins took over and made a brilliant lead up the chimney. He finished in the dark and slept on a tiny ledge. I curled up in the bottom of what I call, for personal reasons, "Mad Dog Chimney" for the most uncomfortable, miserable, suffering night of my life. I was drowning in my own thirst, and my intestines stuck together like last night's noodles. My mouth and throat were too dry to eat, and there wasn't enough water. Ration it. Sip it. Hold it in the mouth until it turns to brine, and then swallow. No comfort there. Sleep eluded. I tossed all night in the bottom of Mad Dog Chimney.

Why had I left Tenaya Lake and Jane?

Discomfort greeted the morning with a mixture of longing and despair. I cleaned the pitch and joined Royal for some fruit cocktail. Happiness is fruit cocktail after a night in Mad Dog Chimney in mid-July.

Some easy climbing brought us to the bolt ladder on the regular route. We had started a hundred feet right of the regular route, and now we would climb this old line until we could cross to the left. Two pitches found us at the big ledges at the base of the Robbins Chimney. No less than 20 empty plastic water bottles and uncountable tins and paper wrappings littered the ledge. Fleeing the pollution, I nutted up a diminishing crack left of the old route. An exhilarating pitch on better rock. I belayed off a tiny ledge on which I found an unmistakable Bridwell topo of Half Dome's regular route.

"You sure we're the first ones up here?"

"Yeah, Man, I'm sure."

From there we were in left-facing dihedrals, whereas the lower part of the climb had been in right-facing ones, which caught the last bits of sun. Cooler now. Cracks filled with vegetation—lush, growing things smelling of rich, green life and water. During belays I buried my nose in these hardier forms of mountain greenery, breathing in the fragrance of organic growth and water. A single leaf of some determined bush held all the wonder and beauty and sadness and creation of the universe. I promised myself that I would lie naked in a meadow by a stream and breathe in the fragrance of paradise, known as earth.

Robbins led up some overhangs to a belay in slings in a dihedral about 50 feet below a huge overhanging flake. Then I followed a thin crack to a point where I placed a marginal Leeper just below the flake. I stood as high as possible to tap the flake. Good. Harder. Solid. I put a long dong behind the flake and hit it twice. A terrifying and indescribable sound stopped everything. Bits of sand fell out from behind the flake.

In a couple of minutes my heart worked enough for me to retreat to the Leeper.

Time to confer with Master Royal.

A tension traverse right got me to another crack. A few pins later the crack thinned to an eighth of an inch wide, twice that deep, crumbling and looking worse above. Time to bolt, one way or another.

"Why don't I have a look at it," my friend said.

"Right on."

I was too far up to be lowered, so I unclipped from the pins in the right crack and began a small pendulum back to the left dihedral. The Leeper pulled as soon as I began, and the next 20 feet down were faster than anticipated.

Royal lowered me, assured us both that I was okay, joked with arid humor about my adventure up there, exchanged belay for lead, and went to it. He took two hours to finish the lead without a bolt, using tiny wired nuts mashed to stay in microscopic cracks. I cleaned a pitch of climbing education or superb climbing, depending.

The sun galloped down as we rappelled a hundred feet into a chimney with two sitting ledges. It looked like rain, but it never materialized. I wanted the sky to drop an ocean, but it gave not a drop. Our high point was about a hundred feet left of where Psyche Flake used to be, and we thought we'd be off the next night. Just two quarts of water for the next day. Body cells collapsed and sticky, mouth cauterized, brain devoted to basics.

Ready by the first morning light after a sleepless night. We jumared to our high point. I led off, tensioning left around a corner to a lovely dirt-moss-grass filled crack a half inch deep and just as wide. After half an hour of severe kidney strain we exchanged leads. Robbins found just the right combination and carried on. Royal led all the last day except for the easy free-climbing to the summit. Hard, intricate climbing. Problems following puzzles, solved through an array of tricks and talents possessed only by a master. Robbins is a supreme rock climber, artist and craftsman. Still competing, but very generous and considerate. A man who, while climbing, knows what he is about, able to concentrate on the immediate detail and the keeping going what must go; to the extent that his being appears as a mystic or a mad scientist, depending.

We reached the summit late in the afternoon, met not by Harding but a beggar chipmunk. Suffering suddenly left. The experience adds to confidence, and the suffering is forgotten in the face of the memory of adventure. No doubt we will suffer again.

On the way down we passed six girls with packs climbing the cables to sleep a night on Half Dome. One was fat and puffing; all clutched the cables like life itself; their adventure was no less than ours. We wished them good night. Further down we ran across three spacy looking fellows with a vicious dog that tore Royal's pants trying to bite him. The owner sidled over, begging pardon, for the dog had had a hard day.

"So have we," Robbins answered, putting his hammer back in its holster.

Cheesecake—Jan at 19,000 feet on Mustagh Ata.   *author's photo*

CHAPTER FIVE

Pain & Peril in the Pamirs

The American Friendship Expedition on Mustagh Ata

The influence of fine scenery, the presence of mountains, appeases our irritations and elevates our friendships.
—R.W. Emerson

THE APPROACH BEGAN IN THE 20TH CENTURY aboard a Japan Airlines 747 at San Francisco's International Airport after a champagne send off arranged by my lovely and charming friend, Leila Kessler, who wished she could go with us.

It ended in the 13th century at 15,000 feet on the side of a central Asian mountain in western China, the realities of Pakistan, Afghanistan and Russia just a few miles away, the ghosts of Marco Polo and Mao even closer.

Nine foul-smelling camels, burdened with our belongings, and four Kirghiz camel drivers, whose lives were both enviously simple and brutally embedded in the middle ages, accompanied us to base camp. None of the Kirghiz desired to go any further. Neither, presumably, did the camels, but a bit of cajoling by the drivers forced the fetid beasts to take a load up to "Camel Camp" at 17,000 feet.

That saved us an enormous amount of load hauling labor on our climb ̇ ̇7 foot Mustagh Ata. "We" were the American Friendship F᠃ ̇rst Americans to climb legally in China for more than ̇ ̇o among the first Westerners allowed in western Specifically, we were Cameron Bangs, 43,

Vermont-born, the elder of our group as well as a doctor, a neophyte world traveler plucked from his Oregon farm and medical practice and plopped down half-way around the world; Ned Gillette, 35, a competitor on the U.S. Nordic Team at the 1968 Olympics, photographer and professional expeditioneer; Jan Reynolds, 24, Ned's young and energetic lady, a Vermonter, a marathon cross-country skier, and, as I found, one tough mountaineer; Galen Rowell, 39, mountaineer, writer, photographer, and possessor of a mind that computes the answer before the question has even been finished; Jo Sanders, Galen's long-time companion of sweet reasonableness, an artist, a travel agent, our director of travel and keeper of base camp; and me, Dick Dorworth, 41, your trusty if eclectic reporter and long time skier and mountaineer.

We were accompanied by Wang Wei-ping, our interpreter, and Chu Ying-hua, our liason officer, who had climbed Mustagh Ata in 1959 and Everest in 1960. The latter climb cost Chu all his toes and his right index finger. Chu is an extraordinary man.

The American Friendship Expedition was an unlikely composition, but destiny has a way of getting life around its own inscrutable reasons. There were nine divorces among us, a remarkable if not entirely upbeat statistic. (A pertinent and slightly more upbeat aside worth contemplating by climbers, partners of climbers, people pondering becoming a partner of a climber, divorce lawyers, and counselors: In the process of reading some of my old journals in connection with writing this book I found this comment made by an ex-wife to a mutual friend, who must have reported it to me and I wrote it down and forgot about it, "The reason Dick is a good skier and climber and writer is the same reason he is impossible to live with." I sent it along to my ex-wife with the comment, "I laughed when I read it, even though it is not funny and very accurate and I thought you would appreciate it." She replied, "I have to laugh as well. I often think I wasn't too insightful when I was younger but this proves there are a few exceptions. Dare you to print it."

I just did.)

In terms of mountaineering and photography, Galen was clearly the most experienced and competent. Ned's skiing credentials were solid, as were my own, and each of us has made it up a few decent climbs. Cam is a well-known physician whose hobbies include climbing and skiing. Jan would not normally have been included on such an endeavor except for the fact that she was Ned's girl. Jo is not a climber or much of a skier; but, in addition to being Galen's lady, Jo worked harder than anyone else without a whole lot of thanks to insure that the American Friendship Expedition made the transition from idea in February to reality in June.

The idea began with Ned. While on a cross-country ski junket to Manchuria that winter, Ned took a shot in the dark and scored the first American permit to climb. The Chinese rightfully assured Ned that Mustagh Ata was the ideal mountain to ski. Four months of frantic activity later, much of it missed by Gillette and Rowell who were ski touring in Pakistan, the red tape was waded through, personnel questions answered, sponsors raised, money gathered, equipment collected, travel arrangements made—and we were in China. Our sponsors were as varied and in some cases as unlikely as the expedition itself—National Geographic, SKI Magazine, The North Face, Beconta, Calvin Klein, Coca-Cola, Budweiser, Nikon, Harold's Club, Mountain Safety Research, Ramer Products, Japan Air Lines, Nike, Smiley Hats, Mother's Nutters, Mountain House, Scott Sports, Mojo Systems, Pendleton and Baush & Lomb.

Climbing in China is complex and multi-faceted, and on all levels no one travels alone to or in the land of Mao. And no one does it cheaply. For the visitor, in fact, China may be the most expensive country on earth. It certainly is for the climber. Our little six week jaunt for six cost a tidy $60,000.

We flew to Peking (Beijing) and spent five days in that ancient, enormous, venerable city, our time fully occupied with sight seeing and exhausting "negotiations" with our hosts, the Chinese Mountaineering Association. "Negotiations" is a polite term the Chinese use for telling visitors exactly what they will and will not be able to do and how much it is going to cost.

To celebrate surviving another round of negotiations, every night we were guests of honor at a banquet highlighted by excellent food, good cheer and innumerable toasts with mao-tai, accurately described by American writer Orville Schell as "a clear liquor that tastes like a mixture of benzene and wood preservative."

From there we flew to the capital of Xinjiang, Urumqi, a drab if bustling city where we spent two days before being allowed on July 4th to go on to Kashgar, China's westernmost city where we celebrated our own country's Independence Day.

In Kashgar we arrived in another and ancient time. More than 2,000 years old, a main stop on the Silk Route, Kashgar is predominately Muslim and largely untouched by time, modern technology, Western thought or the ideology of Karl Marx. As the first westerners most of the people had ever seen, we were surrounded in the streets by hundreds of curious Mongolian faces speaking tongues of Turkish derivation.

Before dawn on the 6th we loaded ourselves and 33 pieces of luggage into a boxlike bus and spent 10 hours getting as close as vehicles can get to Mustagh Ata in the Chinese Pamirs. The road of the old Silk Route, Connecting China and Russia with Pakistan, is a terrible road known as the Karakoram Highway.

(From my notebooks that evening.) The road is incredible. Narrow. Bumpy. Through several tribal cultures. Up huge valleys, mostly barren with scattered oasis' and mud water running high in the rivers and peaks as big as China looming above with great white brightness. Enormous glaciers. All flavored by people living the same as their ancestors have for hundreds of years. Now we are in a lovely green valley with the bus and all our gear piled beside it, a flock of camels, strange people, mules, a Muslim cemetery, moving figures in the distance, our yellow North Face dome tents, and every so often an army truck rolls by. Rising 15,000 feet above us is Mustagh Ata. In the local language 'mus' means ice, 'tagh' means mountain, 'ata' means father. Chu is dressed in his new climbing gear—down parka and Gore-Tex wind pants—and it's 50 degrees.

We spent two days at 10,000 feet before moving up to base camp at

15,000. Thanks to our camel friends—loaded with Kästle skis and barrels of food and packs of gear, an amazing sight—we didn't have to carry loads. I didn't like moving up so fast, but the move was on and nothing to be done about it.

For three days we lived in base camp. Acclimating. Exploring. Hiking to higher elevations. Writing. Reading. Talking.

Having once been sick with pulmonary edema (see 'A Hell of a Climb') from moving too high too fast on a mountain (Denali), I was all for spending at least a week acclimating at base camp. Alas, my wishes were ignored. The push was on.

July 14th dawned cold and cloudy and a storm threatened. Chu said the weather was telling us to stay put for awhile. The American Friendship Expedition held a morning strategy meeting and decided to stay in base camp until the weather improved.

After lunch Jo and Galen left for an afternoon photo hike to the great glacier a few miles south. They no more passed from sight than Ned announced that he and Jan were moving up to Camel Camp at 17,000. Cam and I were invited. Alarmed, I declined, remembering the Dylan line, "It's only other people's games you got to watch out for." On their return, Galen and Jo were surprised, to put it mildly, at the change in plans. Friendship was the theme of our expedition, but by no means could we have been called "The American Cooperation and Communication Expedition." Indeed, friendship, cooperation and communication were sorely stressed and strained and, in some cases, irretrievably broken on the first American expedition to Father Ice Mountain. When the expedition was over Galen and Jo ended their relationship. Galen and Ned never spoke again. I was the only member of the group on speaking terms with every other member of the group by the time we returned to San Francisco International. It took a couple of years for Ned and I to repair our friendship that had been steamrolled by Ned's ambition and his and Galen's contentious rivalry that could have easily cost me my life. I will always be grateful that my friendships with them both were clear and clean by the time Ned was murdered in Pakistan in 1998 and Galen was killed in a plane crash in 2002.

The weather turned to rain with wind, and snowline dropped to just above base camp.

July 14, 1980. A delightful hike with Chu today to the south. On the way we skirted below the glacier. Chu screwed up a roll of film and was despondent. I told him Galen could probably help later. He did. I only meant to give Chu some of my labio-san for his lips, but in the sign-translation confusion he wound up with all of it. So be it. Communication isn't easy in any language. His lips are in terrible shape. On the way back we cut through the center of the glacier which proved to be quite a little adventure. I was surprised at how fast and well Chu moves in the mountains without toes. Cameron thought Chu wouldn't be able to walk to base without mule or camel, but Chu can take good care of himself in these mountains. It may cost him some pain but Chu functions fine.
Galen is not well. Headaches, bad stomach and weak. He has even resorted to codeine, a bad sign.

The next day, the 15th, Galen and I went up in the afternoon, a three-hour climb in marginal weather. Jo, Wang and Chu stayed down. I became aware on that hike that something significant had occurred during or after Galen and Ned's journey to Pakistan and that they were not a healthy match for an expedition, friendship or otherwise. Our mates were out skiing when we arrived at Camel Camp. Galen, feeling better, joined them. While I, feeling whipped beyond the exertions of the day, crawled into a tent and fell asleep. Later, after a hot drink and a meal, I revived. Ned and Jan were energetic, enthusiastic and obviously fit. Galen and Cam were both very tired. Skiing was said to be good and all our gear was working well. In honor of several U.S. ski resorts we frequent, Camel Camp was re-christened "Elevation 17,000." With the help of a stiff dose of vitamin V (Valium) I slept soundly.

The 16th began clear and cold and we were up as the sun arrived. It became a schizophrenic day. We agreed to go up with heavy loads to begin stocking a camp at 19,000 feet. I took more than three hours to haul my allotted cargo to just below a huge ice fall and a perfect site at 19,000, Camp I. The weather was deteriorating. Galen wanted photos of me skiing. I gladly obliged, making my first turns in three months. I had every intention of spending the next few days hauling loads to Camp I, enjoying skiing back down and acclimating at 17,000. Galen's motor drive went through a roll of film before I'd gone 50 yards. None of the others were ready, so I waved and commenced to have the most fun of the entire climb—2,000 vertical feet of untracked, easy snow, powder turning to shallow corn.

When snow ran out I removed my skis and clumped a few hundred yards to Elevation 17,000, three tiny tents perched on a flat spot in the shale slope. The afternoon waned and weather portended foul times. I felt tired but good and looked forward to an earned rest as I fired up a stove for a brew. Twenty minutes later the others arrived with a new, surprising and, to me, totally unacceptable plan—to break camp immediately and move everything up to Camp I.

July 16, 1980. Elevation 17,000. 7 p.m. It is hailing/snowing/blowing. I am in my bag full of warm food and drink. Cameron is outside dictating to himself. Ned, Jan and Galen are humping heavy loads up to Camp I. In the middle of the rush to break camp I remembered my resolve to keep my own counsel on this climb. I simply announced that health demanded another (at least) night here and that I'd keep a tent and move up in the morning. Cam was glad I chose to stay. I'm grateful to have a companion. In my opinion Galen, Ned and Jan are pushing too high too fast too hard, but each to his and her own. Tonight we will increase the valium dosage.

The next morning Dr. Bangs and your reporter, who could not sleep without drugs nor hold food down for very long, broke camp in a beautiful, clear, mountain morning. I carried my skis and reached Camp I in just over two hours. Cam used his skis and took five hours. Jan was sunbathing and puttering around the camp. Ned and Galen had taken loads up to 20,000.

Galen and Ned returned enthusiastic and optimistic about the route above. Ned was obviously the fittest of the group at that point. Galen pre-released four times from his bindings during the day and was both irritated and tired. We spent the rest of the afternoon organizing gear for the planned move up the next day. I had been above base camp just two days and the climb was moving too fast for my system and I knew it. I needed to be at 17,000, but expeditions don't always work according to the needs of individual members. The push was on.

A storm moved in late that afternoon.

July 18, 1980. Camp I. 4 p.m. It has snowed moderately for 24 hours. No signs of letup. I haven't eaten today. One cup of bullion and some water has done it. That and some anti-acid pills Cam gave me to combat the constipation he says could follow the codeine, Tylenol and Valium he gave me to combat the worst headaches I've ever had. Drugs make my head feel better, but I'm a bit slow. If the mind doesn't fail and the body cooperates and the drugs hold out and the weather breaks I think we can climb this thing. My pulse is 64 today. Time for a vitamin V and an attempt at sleep.

Eight hours after writing that I awoke from the codeine-Tylenol-Valium induced grasp of the arms of Morpheus to the realization of acute mountain sickness and previously unimaginable headaches. For several hours I vacillated between passing out, vomiting, defecating, sweating, shivering and losing self-control to pain. Finally, I entered the howling storm of the still dark morning and went to Cameron's tent for help.

Cam's bag of modern medical magic bludgeoned me into a peaceful and painless oblivion for a few hours, but in all things reality must eventually be faced. Galen thought to take my pulse which had climbed from 64 to 88 with no activity. Ned was entering the tent to check on me just as I emerged for a timely vomit. I just missed hitting Ned but my boiling discharge melted a hole in the snow and uncovered a missing ice ax. So, while every cloud does have a silver lining, it was time for me to get off the mountain.

Cam Bangs helps the author prepare to descend from 19,000 on Mustagh Ata.

I got dressed and headed down and July 19, 1980 was among the worst days I've ever known in the mountains, or, really anywhere. Ned accompanied me for a few hundred yards before turning back and leaving me on my own. I do not remember ever feeling so miserable, powerless and vulnerable or less a member of an expedition, a group of friends or, you know, the tribe. Sometime later a doctor friend who saw photos Galen took of me in the tent the day before told me that it was obvious from the face shots that I was suffering from high altitude cerebral edema (HACE). Ten years earlier I had aborted a climb of Denali because of high altitude pulmonary edema (HAPE) and was acutely aware that high altitude climbing was not my strength. In an attempt to overcome (circumvent?) that frailty I had bought a book on how to train for running a marathon, spent 4 months training by the book and then ran the marathon (not very quickly) a few weeks before leaving for China. All that conditioning was not enough to save me from HACE or get me up Mustagh Ata, but it may well have made the difference in getting me down. Several times as I (literally, on a couple of occasions) crawled toward base camp I wanted nothing more than to curl up and go to sleep without giving a shit whether I woke up or not. Had there been warmth and a comfortable bed I may have done just that. But there was neither warmth nor comfort anywhere above base camp in the Pamir Mountains of China and it was a long day. What normally would have taken me 2 or 3 hours to descend took 8. Chu saw from base camp that someone was descending and he met me an hour from camp and accompanied me down to where sweet Jo stuffed me into a sleeping bag inside a tent and filled me with warm fluids and food until I slept the sleep of the grateful to be alive.

The next morning I was better but not well and it was decided that I should return to Kashgar. Accordingly, Wang accompanied me on the hike out to the dirt road known as the Karakoram Highway to seek a ride from one of the rare vehicles passing by. Fortunately, five minutes after we arrived at the road a Chinese Army jeep heading in the right direction stopped and gave me a ride back to Kashgar, elevation 4170 feet, where my health and appreciation of life vastly and quickly improved. Wang returned to base camp.

At the hotel in Kashgar I learned that a British expedition on the way to attempt the first ascent of nearby Kongur Tagh (25,095 feet) was there. I had the great pleasure of knocking on the door of my friend Chris Bonington, leader of the expedition who had no idea I was in China and, when he opened the door, saying, "Mr. Bonington, I presume?" We had a great visit and it was refreshing to see a familiar, friendly face after getting off Mustagh Ata. (Bonington's team failed on Kongur Tagh that year but returned the next to complete the first ascent.)

Meanwhile, on the morning of July 20th my mates on Mustagh Ata moved up to Camp II at over 20,000 feet. They broke trail on their mountaineering skis through two feet of fresh snow. The weather was not good. The new snow added to the exertion of the day. Everyone was tired at the end of the day and Cam elected to go no higher. Very early on the 21st Ned, Galen and Jan made their summit bid, committing themselves to more than 4,000 vertical feet of climbing in a single day. They took no bivouac gear, setting an 8 p.m. deadline to either reach the summit or retreat.

Late in the day Jan began to falter and move more slowly than her partners. She dropped back and vomited several times, an unpleasant experience and one of the more obvious announcements of the dangers of altitude sickness. Nevertheless, Jan kept on with the climber's penance—putting one foot in front of the other.

During most of the climb Ned had broken trail, a remarkable testimony to his endurance and determination, but an effort that took a physical toll. Late in the day Jan broke trail for short periods, and it was this effort that accelerated her deterioration. The pace was slowing and time was running out.

Galen, who pushes himself harder than most hard drivers I know, was not at his optimum health at any time on Mustagh Ata. Nevertheless, he's awesomely stubborn with a goal in mind and sight. Fearing that the slow pace of the group might destroy any chance for the summit, Galen decided to push ahead as fast as he could, alone. It was about 8 p.m., the group's self-imposed deadline, and they estimated they were about 500 vertical feet from the summit. They ignored the deadline.

Galen dropped his pack, gave his water bottles to the others, and reached the summit alone not long before 9 p.m. He took a self portrait, looked around for a few minutes in the biting cold and increasing wind at a darkening Russia in the distance. Then he began his descent, passing Ned and Jan on the way.

A half hour later Ned and Jan reached the top. Considerations at that isolated place and time: The satisfaction of fine accomplishment. Fatigue. Cold. Danger. The ethereal beauty of a high mountain sunset. The rapidly spreading darkness. Photographic obligations to sponsors, professionalism and posterity. Camp II with its shelter so far below.

Nevertheless, the main objective was the ski down in fresh powder in fading light. As Ned wrote in National Geographic: *"More than the summit, we seek the thrill of skiing down, of floating across this immensity in hauntingly perfect snow."* After only a few minutes at the top they started down, stopping often to catch their breath in the slim atmosphere.

Mustagh Ata is the highest mountain ever skied from its summit. Jan Reynolds is the first woman to ski at such altitudes. I do not know of any mountain that high climbed that fast, proving that skis are a most effective tool in many mountaineering situations. It would have been impossible to reach the summit in one day from Camp II without skis. And Jan could have been in serious trouble if her skis had not allowed her to descend so quickly.

A week later both Jan and Galen showed obvious signs of the hardships of the climb. Ned, on the other hand, appeared to have breezed through it all as if it hadn't happened. They unanimously agreed that the two-day descent, with 8,000 vertical feet of skiing, was incredibly fine and worth every bit of time and effort it took.

And I missed it, damnit.

Sean Peterson in the Owens River Gorge   *photo Susan Morning*

CHAPTER SIX

Human Time in the Owens River Gorge

IT IS DECEPTIVE, CALIFORNIA's OWENS RIVER GORGE, a deep gash
in the earth narrow enough that it is invisible from a hundred yard away,
in places less. In geologic time the Gorge is not so old, formed between
600,000 and 100,000 years ago by the draining of the enormous
Pleistocene Lake, formed, in turn, by the abundant volcanic activity that
marks the history and potential future of the Mammoth Mountain area
on the east side of the Sierra Nevada. Crowley Lake, which sits on the
site of the ancient Pleistocene Lake, is not a remnant of the older and
larger one; it is a creation of the desires of man rather than the mandates
of nature. Unless one is a Creationist (in which case one should read no
further, if one is able to read at all), the Gorge is a relative newcomer to
the geology of earth. In human time, of course, the Owens River Gorge is
ancient, though its present incarnation as a place for humans to recreate
was entirely man made less than a hundred years ago.

The present Owens River Gorge was formed from man's deceit,
greed and empire building and the delusion of unlimited growth which
Ed Abbey pointed out is the ethic of the cancer cell. The Gorge we know
today is a by-product of the (so far) unlimited growth of Los Angeles
and of the deceptions of a handful of developers, boosters, politicians,
city and federal employees, engineers and political appointees working
on behalf of that growth. Among them were William Mulholland,
Gifford Pinchot, J.B. Lippencott, Fred Eaton and the President of the
U.S., Teddy Roosevelt. It is a too well known to repeat here, oft-told and,

sadly, old story, as old as man. A fertile Owens Valley and the roaring Owens River, together forming a paradise of sorts, were dried up to water the concrete gridlock of road rage, smog, pollution and over population that characterizes southern California. In the interests of efficiency and evaporation control, the vital Owens River was diverted into a huge steel pipe running more than 200 miles south to Los Angeles.

In due, not even geologic, time this, too, will pass.

Meanwhile, until the water from the pipe is returned to the river (not likely in the lifetimes of anyone reading this), the thousand foot deep gash in the desert has become a Mecca for rock climbers. When you turn east off Highway 395 near the bottom of Sherwin Grade just north of Bishop and drive a couple of miles and see the huge pipe above the high desert mostly treeless landscape you are very close. Look for the pipe. I had long wanted to see and climb in the Gorge, but for various reasons it never happened. Then, on an April day while on a climbing trip with my buddy Sean Peterson we finally got there. The first morning we went to Wilson's Sporting Goods in Bishop to buy a guide book, but it was out of stock and out of print until the author updates it. Wilson's let us copy enough pertinent pages to find our way into the Gorge and up enough routes to keep us busy for more time than we had. In the company of our old Bishop friend, Sierra Club Books "Simple Foods for the Pack" authoress, earth-mother and pathfinder Claudia Axcell, we found the Central Gully trail at the end of a dirt road. A huge power line above emitted an unsettling, incessant hum that made me not want to spend too much time in close proximity.

We had been warned that the Central Gully trail was "5th class trail walking" and so it was, but we enjoyed the hand painted sign at the top:

> Please
> Keep on trail
> No Trundling
> Respect DWP
> No posing
> Thanks

DWP is the Los Angeles Department of Water and Power which owns the Owens River Gorge. It is affectionately, or not, known as "Dwip" and we do respect it. As always, we stuck to the path while and avoided trundling and posing. As expected, the trail is not for the unfit, the clumsy, the inattentive or the seeker of pleasurable hiking. In half an hour we reached the bottom and hundreds of high quality climbing routes, many of them above our abilities. For a couple of old (again, the relativity of time) climbers this was wonderful. Sean, 43 at the time, grew up in Ketchum, Idaho where we both live, and is a fine climber/ skier/mountaineer. A graduate of the CIA (New York's Culinary Institute of America), Sean is a chef *extraordinaire* both on the road and in the kitchen and a very disciplined, skilled and determined man. Ten years ago Sean had a terrible climbing accident in Idaho's Sawtooth Mountains which nearly cost him his life and left him in a coma. When he woke up he had to learn to talk, walk, climb, ski, play the guitar, sing, work, collect wild mushrooms, think, feel and live all over again. Since then he has pursued life with renewed appreciation and enthusiasm for this world's transient pleasures, sufferings, and abiding human meaning. For instance, as a birthday gift to himself on his full moon 40th birthday Sean started at 5 p.m. after the ski lifts closed and climbed up and skied down Sun Valley's Bald Mountain five times before dawn when he quit and had breakfast. Baldy is 3200 vertical feet. Sean is a superior climbing partner, road chef, campfire balladeer, companion, fellow Buddhist and friend.

As always these days, I am the elder among all my climbing companions (66 at the time). As a gift to myself on my 40th birthday, more than a third of a life ago, I ran my first and next-to-last marathon, a piece of cake compared to 16,000 vertical in a night. Still, Sean and I understand some things about each other, and we leapt upon the walls of polished, steep volcanic tuff with enthusiasm, pleasure, and the excitement of climbing in a new area.

While non-climber Claudia sat in the sun (and shade) sketching and writing in her journal, Sean and I worked our way through and up some of the best rock routes in America. Climbing grades, like time and age are relative concepts, but when we're climbing well Sean is able to safely lead most hard 5.10 and easy 5.11 routes, while I can usually lead easier 5.10s. We started with a 5.8 route on the aptly named "Warm Up Wall" and were immediately reminded of the relative merits of ratings. We had been climbing in Idaho's City of Rocks where the granite is both rougher (i.e. stickier) and the routes less steep and artsy-craftsy fancy footwork takes pressure off the arms and fingers. Not so with the smooth STEEP climbing in the Gorge. Even easier routes pumped our feeble old arms and fragile old psyches and encouraged rest between routes. At the end of the first day, while we were hiking back up the trail to the *no posing* sign and humming power lines I noticed I couldn't make a fist, so trashed were my forearms and fingers.

Still, we persevered. Over the next week we managed five days climbing and one rest day of excellent skiing at Mammoth in the company of old friends Robin and Jim Morning and John and Lynette Armstrong. We got a taste and learned enough of the climbing and the place, with its remnant signs of industrial presence—a road, mineshafts, old power stations, huge eye-hooks drilled deep into rock, random pieces of rusted machinery—that we will be back. We found great camping in the pinions nearby. There are too many fine routes to climb in this lifetime. The best and hardest one we got up in good style is a classic with the politically/socially provocative name "Sendero Luminoso." But my favorite place because of its several moderate routes that I could climb without terror and fatigue paralyzing my limbs and will was the Great Wall of China, with routes named "Child of Light," "Heart of the Sun," Fortune Cookie," "Enter the Dragon," and "Tsing Tao." At the Great Wall, some 40 or 50 vertical feet above the bottom of the gorge is the sand from the beaches of the old Owens River at high water. It's a good place to hang out. We discovered the southern entrance (paved) road below a locked gate that is a longer but far gentler access. We were delighted by the abundance of life and greenery and the microenvironment that has grown up around the stream that was once a mighty river capable of carving a gorge. In response to a series of law suits and decades of dissatisfaction from the citizens of the Owens River Valley, in 1991, after 50 years of barrenness, Dwip began letting water back into the gorge, which it calls "… the Department's premier restoration program."

That law-suit-inspired restoration program has created a lovely place for climbers, hikers, fishermen, birds, reptiles, rodents and those interested in watching, photographing or writing about any of these exotic creatures. A geologist could amuse himself for 600,000 years down there. It is a place to recommend support, as are the law suits that restored it.

One day we had finished climbing and were getting organized at the bottom of the Central Gully trail for the hike out when we were astonished by the sight of three huge middle-aged men coming down the path. They seem to me a metaphor for humanity and nature, for southern California and the Owens River Gorge, for man's desire to control and thus make abstract the environment we all live from and within. It was late in the opening day of fishing season. These three fishermen had never been into the Gorge and had just driven from Los Angeles to cast their baits upon its waters. They had obviously had a very difficult time getting down the trail, and there was no way they could get back out before dark, even if they turned around without baiting a hook or casting a fly. The first two I estimate at 50 to 60 lbs overweight, trying to use their fishing poles as walking sticks and anxious to get to the water. They appeared very tired and annoyed but managed cheerful small talk with me and Sean. One of them slipped on the loose rocks of the trail and went down hard enough to alarm us. He got back up, bruised, scraped and embarrassed. He laughed. "Obviously, I don't know what I'm doing and don't belong here," he said before heading down to the stream. Their partner was a bit behind. He was approximately 80 to 100 lbs overweight, panting like a racehorse and sweating like an approaching heart attack. He was one uncomfortable fisherman, though he, too, maintained cheerfulness. "I'll never be able to climb back up that trail," he said, stating the obvious with a self-deprecating chuckle. We agreed and recommended the longer south route up a gentler incline. The out-of-shape, overweight, L.A. fisherman who lived on the water of the Owens River had finally visited its source, and he headed to the stream to join his buddies.

Sean and I hiked out to the rim. The next day when we returned there was no sign of the fishermen. They either managed to get themselves out or the spirits of the Owens River Gorge abducted them into the purgatory of unlimited growth and eternal 5th class hiking where they are doomed, like Sisyphus, who betrayed the knowledge of the gods, to endless, fruitless, ultimately unsatisfying labor. At any rate, it is a good bet they won't be back to the Owens River Gorge in the relatively near future.

But we will.

The author on Mt. Steele.   *photo Jeannie Wall*

CHAPTER SEVEN

Climbing Steele with Lady J

LADY J IS A REAL PISSER. That's fact and *double entendre*, but I won't explain except that once Lady J gets going on something she extracts the last drop from herself, and you ignore her energy and its direction at your peril. Lady J is my girl friend, but she refuses to let me use her name in this account. You'll have to ask her exactly why. She's a queen among women and I'd do anything for her, including choosing a pseudonym to protect her anonymity in print, her reputation among readers too rigid to embrace unorthodox relationships, and the private process of stripping away the layered guilt of a recovering Catholic from public scrutiny about what she is doing with me. So, while she's certainly not unknown among our friends, Lady J it is. She is tough and lovely, ambitious and fun, smart and funny, and a good climber. She is so very beautiful to me.

Lady J was invited to climb Mt. Steele in the Yukon and she asked me to join her. In addition to the harsh reality that she is an accomplished endurance athlete whose skill and ability to move long, fast and confidently in mountains exceeds my own in all but a few technical situations, there is the more severe truth that I am 61 years old and she but 32. It takes competence, effort and attention to climb a peak like Steele, and Lady J moves in the mountains with the speed of an ultra-runner. I can move as fast but not so long, or as long but not so fast. We have our challenges together but I would go anywhere with her, and to climb in the Yukon is a gift, a joy and an experience not to miss.

There is climbing history there and more in the making. Besides, the way it's been, is, and most likely will remain for an indeterminate time, if I weren't climbing in the Yukon in spring I'd be climbing somewhere else. Why not Steele with Lady J?

But climbing Steele with Lady J was, for me, as much about Lady J as about Steele, giving this climb a different flavor than most. Mt. Steele is in the St. Elias Mountains of Canada's Yukon Territory, though it is most easily accessed from Alaska. It is in the Kluane National Park and is named after Sam Steele, the most famous Canadian Mounted Policeman of his day. Sam Steele was called "The Lion of the Yukon" for his successful efforts to bring order and law to the undomesticated, lawless and often chaotic frontier of western Canada in the late 19th century. He was described as a friend to Sitting Bull, the great Sioux Chief, and the Queen of England. He later served with distinction as Commander of Lord Strathcona's Horse in the Boer War. One description of Steele in Africa reads, "Fighting Sam and his Big Stirrups rode the veldt as they had the Canadian prairie." In actuality, Fighting Sam and his Big Stirrups riding the veldt conjures up a majestic image of noble warriors masking a depraved and brutal reality of the Boer War, of every war, of war itself. It was said they exacted six Boer casualties for every one of their own. The Strathcona's Horse was the most dreaded among the Boers as Steele's troops were known for their ferocity. Steele's biographer, Robert Stewart, reports, "They were said to have lynched Boer prisoners, and when a British staff officer remonstrated, they offered to lynch him, too." Sam Steele, like the mountain named after him, was not to be taken lightly nor approached with an expectation of great warmth, and we did not.

The literature offers some different heights for Mt. Steele. The highest I've seen is 16,664, the lowest 16,440. Steele is located in the midst of some of the wildest, most lovely, inhospitable, glaciated mountain terrain on earth. It is the 10th highest mountain in North America, including the three big volcanoes near Mexico City. It is the 5th of Canada's highest peaks, all of them in the St. Elias Mountains, the tallest being Mt. Logan at 19,540 feet. The St. Elias Mountains are a major element of the Pacific Mountain Systems of the North America Cordillera between Latitude 59 and 62 degrees North, and Longitude 137 and 142 degrees West. The range comprises several other ranges forming a shallow arc some 300 miles long and 150 miles wide between the Gulf of Alaska and the Yukon Plateau.

Mt. Steele was first climbed by the East Ridge in August 1935 by Walter and Harrison Wood, Joseph Fobes and Hans Fuhrer. They used 38 pack and saddle horses and had the primary goal of establishing triangulation control for a subsequent aerial survey; but, in addition to several spurs, buttresses and ridge crests climbed in pursuit of the work at hand, a couple of noteworthy summits were climbed just because they were there. Mt. Steele was the most significant. That their work prepared them for the endeavor is evidenced in the fact that they climbed up and came down the 9000 vertical foot ridge in one day. Many modern climbers seeking first ascents solicit sponsorships or write articles and books or make TV films of their adventures in order to support their climbing addiction. In earlier days many climbers sought jobs that would take them to where the mountains of their obsessions stand. The 1935 climb of Steele was the last recorded ascent of a major peak of the St. Elias Mountains in which aircraft played no part. It would be unthinkable for any but the most eccentric modern climber to forego the convenience and speed of air travel for the purity of intention required walking to the base of a climb in the St. Elias range. The modern world has managed to pervert even time into a commodity instead of a blessing. In 1964, however, after being flown into Mt. Logan, the first party to climb the formidable Independence Ridge (among the group was my good friend and climbing partner David Stelling) took 8 days carrying 120 pound packs (including 220 cm. Kneissl downhill skis which probably weighed 15 pounds) to walk and ski out 120 miles from the mountain to Haines Junction on the Alaska Highway; and the fine American climber Jack Roberts skied around the huge massif (the largest on earth, I believe) of Mt. Logan in 1990.

Climbing Mt. Steele is neither technically nor objectively the most ambitious or hazardous of mountaineering challenges. Nor is it close to the limits of what the hardest routes demand of leading climbers today, but it is a classic alpine endeavor. The indomitable and peerless American climber, Fred Beckey, has written of the sort of climbing we would find on Steele, "Most alpine undertakings in Alaska do not involve cragging, but represent committing teamwork, often involving a certain risk. Mountaineering here represents a grand human adventure in one of the most diverse regions imaginable....Alaskan climbing, with some notable exceptions, seldom requires great athletic skill; gallantry can usually be obtained easier in other lands. And while technical skill and physical strength are absolute requirements for certain routes, good judgment and perseverance are equally important, and often more so.... it is the crossing of glaciers that can provide a special catalog of horrors. All glaciers are not created equal: some are classified as temperate, others polar. Alaska has both, and some have internal characteristics of both types. Negotiating the countless stretch marks on a large Alaskan glacier is often the most vexing and frightening aspect of a mountain adventure."

In 1998 Lady J climbed Mt. Logan. While on that climb she met and befriended two Alaskan climbers, Paul Barry and Dave Hart, both engineers in the North Slope oil fields. For each of the past eight years the two of them have set their climbing sights on difficult peaks in Alaska and Canada. They are strong, focused, and as efficiently precise as engineers in their climbing. Usually, but not always, together, they have climbed more than 20 Alaskan/Canadian peaks over 12,000 feet, 10 of them over 15,000. Hart climbed Denali (20,320) without Barry, a third generation Alaskan whose family carved a living with sweat and steadfastness out of the wild bush and hard rock of the Alaskan frontier, and the Barry family tradition of perseverance is evident in Paul's climbing. Dave Hart interrupted a year long round-the-world traveling sabbatical from the oil fields to return to Alaska for his annual foray with Barry. For the spring of 2000 they chose Mt. Lucania (17,150 feet) and Mt. Steele for no better (nor, certainly, worse) reason than that they were next on the hit list.

And they invited Lady J.

And she invited me.

We decided to begin with the west face of Steele, first climbed in

1937 by Bradford Washburn and Bob Bates, both legendary American mountaineers. They made the second ascent by a new route on Steele after making the first ascent of Lucania (at the time the highest unclimbed peak in North America) not because they were seeking another new route or were interested in second ascents, but because unusually warm conditions made it impossible for their plane to return and pick them up. They were stranded in the wildest part of the Yukon with no other transportation than their feet and personal resources. To get out, they decided that after climbing Lucania they would climb the west face of Steele in order to descend the route of the 1935 Wood expedition to Burwash Landing, 60 miles to the east. Both Washburn and Bates wrote excellent accounts of their month long adventure, including this wonderful line of Washburn's: "The conviction that anything Walter Wood could get up we could get down buoyed our spirits." He was proved right, as conviction so often is, but my own state of mind approaching the same mountain 63 years after them was less buoyant.

I was climbing with three strong climbers nearly 30 years my junior, two of whom I'd never met, and I had my own justifiable and phantom insecurities about the enterprise. The unpretentious terror that goes with negotiating the stretchmarks of glaciers is not my favorite part of mountaineering. Carrying heavy loads is not my strong suit as a climber, nor was it ever. My hands and feet have been abused by repeated exposure to cold and my own carelessness for so long that their circulatory systems are, to put it mildly, dangerously sluggish and painfully slow. And altitude has been my mountain nemesis in the past. A combination of improper preparation and twice being in expedition situations where I was presented with the choice of quitting the climb at hand or climbing too high too fast, resulted in altitude sickness for me. I've had both pulmonary and cerebral edemas. They are life-threatening, uncomfortable, debilitating, frightening, and ruin an otherwise good climb. While 16,000 feet is not very high in the comparative world of mountaineering, it is high enough, and cerebral edema is not a comparative experience. I was happy to be with Lady J and thrilled about the climbing; but paranoia concerning death, failure, being an idiot and hindrance to my climbing partners was part of my pre-expedition state of mind.

What if my lungs filled up with fluids and I didn't have the breath to speak my mind? What if my brain cavity filled up with fluids and squeezed my brain cells to the size of a pea, leaving me not enough judgment to breathe? What if my cerebellum was already the size of a pea? What if I ran out of both breath and brains? What if I couldn't keep up? What if I disappointed Lady J? What if Dave and Paul thought I was a weak old fool and didn't like me? What if I was a weak old fool and we couldn't work together on the mountain? What if I fell in a crevasse? What if my hands froze and fell off? What if ... ? What if ... ?

Stephen Stills and Buffalo Springfield sang it so well:

"Paranoia strikes deep/Into your life it will creep...."

I learned long ago that being able to recognize my own paranoia and doubts doesn't mean there is nothing of substance to be paranoid and doubtful about. But being aware of dangers and possibilities and fears is a completely different matter than letting them control your mind and rule your life. Fear, like fire, is a friend who gives warm advice and information; but it's destructive to let it burn near the great forests of reality when the winds of imagination blow. Fear as an operating premise of living is unacceptable except to true believers of certain religions and those for whom image is everything. Keeping one's own counsel and watching the phantoms of doubt pass through the mind without grabbing hold of them is a requisite skill of climbing and, for that matter, all of life. For the most part, though not completely, before going to Alaska I actually thought that all would be fine, the climb would go well and I would climb Steele if any of us did. But to deny the phantoms' potential for sabotage would make this an incomplete and inaccurate accounting. Most of all I wanted to have a fine and memorable time climbing with Lady J.

Otherwise, what's the point of suffering up a 16,664 foot mound of snow and ice in the middle of nowhere? Because it's there?

We arrived in Anchorage in the early afternoon of April 21, 2000, met by our friend Marcie Baker and her two daughters. We spent a frenetic afternoon shopping for food and last minute pieces of equipment and packing for an expedition. Then dinner with Marcie and John Baker and family and early to bed. Up at 2 a.m. on the 22nd. Paul and Dave show up at 2:30 for the five hour drive to Chitna where our flight to the Yukon would begin. Dave and Paul are both big men on the order of NFL wide receivers with the lean sculpted look of lots of training and the gleeful enthusiasm and wild eyes of the adventurer before the hard work sets in, or, perhaps, receivers juking linebackers while contemplating the whereabouts of the safety. They are immediately comfortable and easy to like. By the time we reached the dirt air strip at Chitna the bonds of committing teamwork were already being forged.

An hour after we arrived, a small, powerful plane, a Beaver, appeared out of the southern sky and landed. The pilot, Paul Claus, stepped out and greeted Lady J, Paul and Dave, old friends from previous climbs. He and I were introduced. We quickly loaded the plane for the hour flight to Claus' compound on the Chitna River, the Ultima Thule Lodge. Claus has the deserved reputation of being the best of the modern Alaskan mountain pilots. He and his father and mother and wife run Ultima Thule Lodge. From there, Claus and his father, John, fly climbers, skiers and hunters into mountain and bush locations of extreme inaccessibility and great majesty, places where even 38 pack and saddle horses would be worse than useless. Claus has the reputation of flying climbers the highest and nearest to their routes, skiers to the top of the choicest runs and hunters closest to the trophy game of their dreams. His wife, Donna, has described Claus as the Van Gogh of flying, referring, one presumes, to his professional artistry with a plane rather than to personal neuroses. Flying with Claus is a bargain, thrill, pleasure and education. On the flight in we saw a wolf and then half a mile away a grizzly. It was the first and, at this writing, only grizzly I've ever seen. Claus dropped down and circled the huge bear only a hundred feet away. The grizzly ran and looked up at the plane and was clearly and understandably disturbed and unhappy, though it was beautiful to watch. From the safety of the plane, it was viscerally clear where grizzly and man are on the food chain. One would not with impunity disturb a creature like this if the grizzly was up close and on equal footing.

Claus decided that suspect weather dictated that we spend a night at the lodge. The next morning he began to shuttle us in, a two hour round-trip flight. Dave and Paul went first. While we waited we had the opportunity to talk with and get to know the fine Swiss climber/skier/photographer, Reudi Homberger, Claus' good friend. Homberger is well known in the mountain world, and I was delighted to meet him. We spoke of mutual friends, particularly the late great skier Roger Staub and the clothing magnate Yvon Chouinard, and of our common love for mountains. Inspired by Claus, Homberger is learning to fly, and he spoke of the necessity throughout life of continuing to discover, to challenge the mind and spirit and body, to constantly stretch the limits of personal possibilities, and to faithfully live near the edge where the most action and information can be found. It was a good conversation to take into Steele, and I thought often of Homberger during the climb.

Claus returned. He was able to get our partners up to 9400 feet on the Dennis Glacier. This was more than 2000 vertical feet, several miles and countless stretch marks closer to the climb than Washburn and Bates had gotten. Another party of three was also going to Steele to try a route on snowshoes from the south. Because Claus had landed and taken off and was comfortable with conditions on the glacier, they joined Lady J and me for the flight, all of us and all our gear jammed like sardines into the heavily loaded plane. Steele goes years without seeing a climber, so another expedition starting the same day was unexpected. At one point during the flight Claus gave us a little bump to announce we had crossed from Alaska to Canada. Outside the plane at 10,000 feet it was minus 10 degrees Fahrenheit at one in the afternoon. We flew over the glaciers and rock and snow of unimaginably beautiful mountains and quite believable difficulties and suffering for those who wish to climb them.

By the time we landed, Paul and Dave had dug the requisite wind protected walled site in the snow and assembled their tent. We were in the middle of the glacier, surrounded on three sides by high walls of snow, ice, and rock. The small pyramid-like summit of Steele was visible to the northeast 7000 vertical feet and uncountable steps away. Endless glacier fell away to the southwest. We unloaded the plane. Claus took off with the agreement to return in two weeks. The snowshoe expedition moved a hundred yards away out of sight. We didn't talk with them again until the climb was over. Lady J and I dug our own protected platform and put up the tent. We ate lunch and briefly enjoyed the scenery before the work commenced. Dave and Paul went first, choosing a route up the glacier and marking it with wands to guide the return, hauling their loads in sleds. We used mountaineering skis, boots and bindings (and overboots designed to keep feet reasonably warm in minus 40 degrees Fahrenheit temperatures). Lady J and I carried our loads in packs on our backs. Because we did not have to pick the route, place wands, drag sleds, be the first to contemplate this glacier's particular catalog of horrors, and because we have spent a lot more of our lives on skis than have our mates, we overtook them long before the second camp site. It was the last time we would overtake Paul and Dave. Even in their tracks, carefully plotted around the obvious and latent double-edged crevasses stretching everywhere, the snow around us periodically settled with a soft-sounding whuuump. This momentarily stopped the heart and injected a shot of adrenaline into the system. In its own way, this took more energy than the loads we carried.

We left a cache at 10,000 feet at the base of the steep buttress we would climb and skied back to the first camp in northern evening light of the long Yukon days of late April. Without sleds, Lady J and I had an enjoyable three mile ski back down the tracks on the gently sloping glacier. Even moving quite fast, the snow at intervals settled with a subtle drop and a feather soft sound triggering the adrenal glands. It was the last 'fun' skiing of the trip.

That night I wrote in my journal:

Still light and so amazingly beautiful—miles of glaciers, seracs, huge ice falls, crevasses everywhere. But it is minus 10 degrees F to minus 20 degrees F at the moment at 9400 feet. Too cold to go high. It was warm when we landed and stayed that way until the sun dropped.

I am happy here with Lady J. In the tent. On the glacier. Away from the madding crowd. Life is so simple, so harsh, so clean and lovely and full of consequence for the slightest attitude of frivolity.

The best part of climbing is the places it gets you to, geographically on the outside, in all dimensions inwardly. One attraction of the geography of climbing is its distance from the most obvious wounds of man's unrelenting assault on the natural world. They are further away in the Yukon than in the Yosemite Valley which has unrivaled climbing but, like Yellowstone and other failures of the National Park Service, has more in common with Disneyland, corporate boardrooms and fast food economics than with wilderness, biological integrity or natural experience and healthy relationships with Mother Earth. It is no coincidence that as the collective unconsciousness of humankind contemplates the man-caused disintegration of the natural biology of earth, places like Everest, Denali, Rainier, Shasta, Mt. Blanc, the Grand Teton, Kilimanjaro and Whitney have become congested, covered with garbage, the antithesis of wild, natural geography. Though some climbers climb for ego and self-promotion rather than for transformative experience and education, I believe that underneath those surface and destructive motivations is a search for connection with the earth. Attentive and aware climbers make that link. While every climber is not conscious or concerned with the biologic world through with he moves, I agree with Jack Turner who writes, "I do not believe it is an accident that many leaders of modern conservation and bioregional movements—John Muir, David Brower, Arne Naess, George Sessions, Gary Snyder—have been mountaineers." Climbing is not a frivolous activity, and it offers the faithful a perspective on life and the earth and one's relationship with each that is clearer than that seen from the valleys.

By the time we slept it had been a long Easter Sunday.

The significance of weight changes when carried on your own back. It's fascinating how all the items of food and clothing, literature and convenience, that seemed so essential in Anchorage and Bozeman and Ketchum get left at the first camp. We each brought three books to get us through storms, but only one with the engaging title "Sleeping, Dreaming and Dying", made it into our packs. We discarded an entire layer of clothes. Lady J reduced our food rations to a lean diet of about 1000 calories a day, far less than what we burned. I am a vegetarian and Lady J monitors food with a wary eye for taste, performance and low-fat efficiency. On this expedition she was a gourmet cook of healthy, svelte cuisine comprised of oat meal, couscous, packaged pasta, powdered potatoes, nuts, cheese, chocolate, tea and coffee. Dave and Paul have a different approach, eating the processed food of mainstream America in mind boggling amounts that would have broken my back. They ate with gusto wonderful to behold, suffering no visible ill effects, from their huge packs of freeze dried dinners, Oreo cookies, pop tarts, candy bars and bagels with cream cheese. Dave even carried a pound of Velveeta cheese. I was amazed. Nevertheless, a week later Lady J and I devoured with relish their care packages of food laced with unpronounceable chemicals that we would not dream of eating in the civilized world. We drew the line at Velveeta, but those Oreos tasted great.

On the morning of the 24th, leaving behind a large stash of fuel, food, books and a spare tent, we all pulled sleds and carried packs and slowly moved back up to the second camp. Again we dug sites and assembled tents. We ate a snack before ferrying loads up to Camp 3. This is where being able to move as long but not as fast or as fast but not as long began to show its challenges. After gaining perhaps 400 vertical feet in a half mile on skis it was necessary to exchange skis for crampons. We began kicking steps up a steep, soft snow field that led to the crest of the ridge. It was arduous work. Plant ice ax. Step. Step. Plant ice ax. Step. Step. Plant ice ax. Step. Step. Repeat for hours with the rhythms of eternity. My pack probably weighed 60 pounds, about a pound a year, but it felt like a hundred, as did I. Every step took an effort that all my training seemed not to have prepared me for. Step. Step. The weight of an endless snow slope pressed down, growing heavier. The others moved ahead. I followed. Step. Step. Plant ice ax. Step. Step. When carrying loads, perseverance is strategy, friend and saving grace. The first day of mountain suffering is always the hardest. I know it will get better. Still, as expected, I am the slowest and I suffer alone, kicking steps, taking breaths, moving up. I smile at the adage "Climbing is a metaphor for life." Step. Step. Inhale. Exhale. Step. Step. Suffer. Suffer. That's life today. It is the climber's version of the Zen maxim, "Chop wood, carry water." Step. Step. Suffer. Suffer.

I gain the ridge crest. It drops a thousand feet off the other side. The ridge is mixed rock and snow, easier going, only a few feet from the precipice, a nasty place in a whiteout. The others are ahead. I keep moving. By the time I see them digging a platform for Camp 3 at around 12,400 feet I was tired and moving slow. When I was about 400 feet below them an angel, Lady J, miraculously appeared from above like a gift of boundless compassion with a laugh and a kiss and her empty pack, all of which she gave to me. She took my thousand pound pack and carried it up to the cache. I headed down, relieved, grateful and very happy. By the time we got back to Camp 2 I was thrashed and trashed and in serious need of fluids, as were Paul, Dave and Lady J. We ate and drank and then slept with gratefulness.

The weather held so we moved to Camp 3 early on the 25th, leaving a small cache at Camp 2. It was a repeat of the previous day except the track was in and familiar ground is psychologically easier. We stepped across and skirted several visible crevasses, and surely there were others crossed on merciful bridges of snow. Again, I was slowest. Twice during the day that same angel descended from above and carried my pack up crucial sections. As a consequence of her help I arrived at Camp 3 less wasted than the day before. But Lady J was far more fatigued than she should have been. In climbing, as in all life, carrying too much weight too long breaks down even the strongest. If we had gone at my pace we would have moved slower, made more carries between camps, and assumed a higher risk of being stopped by changing weather. At their pace I needed help carrying loads. Though I was and am grateful for Lady J's efforts on my behalf, I do not want to jeopardize her goals or for her to neglect her abilities.

That night we discussed the situation and our options. After three consecutive hard days carrying loads I needed a break. We wanted to reach the summit together, so Lady J suggested that I rest a day while they ferry loads up to camp 4 at 14,100 on the big plateau between Lucania and Steele, a proposal I embraced and to which Dave and Paul agree.

April 26 is warm and they leave early. I wrote in my journal,

It was cold in the night. My feet never warmed......Neither of us hydrated enough. It is snowing slightly off and on, though the clouds are thin and it is bright. Visibility fluctuates. No wind. Very quiet and peaceful......This place is amazing in all directions. Glaciers that run for miles. Seracs. Ice falls. Mountains. Vast snow fields. Huge rock/ice/snow walls, sometimes shrugging off temporary snow and ice with a roar and a show. Including the three snowshoers, there are probably not 20 people within 40 air miles of here.

I spent the day resting, hydrating, jotting in my journal, reading, napping, filling all the containers with water from melted snow, enjoying the scenery. My body was grateful beyond measure.

They took four hours to reach the plateau and a bit over two hours to get back down. Paul led and reported intricate and difficult route finding on blue ice thinly covered with snow, many crevasses, and huge cubistic ice blocks the size of ten story buildings tilted above the steep slopes that needed crossing. Eventually, each block will move. Very beautiful. Very hard. The whole achieved step by step. Step. Step. Plant ice ax. Stay alert. Be aware. Danger everywhere.

The day of rest made all the difference for me.

The next day, the 27th, we moved up in fine weather, using crampons, carrying skis. The climbing involved hard ice, across steep snow slopes and under blocks that we hoped were as solid as they looked. For those few steps of our lives they were. With the route in it took only three hours to reach the camp site on the plateau at about 14,100 feet. Lady J and I on one rope easily kept up with Dave and Paul on another. I arrived feeling strong and good and confident about the climb, thanks to the extra rest and my companions' fine efforts. My hands were a problem, as expected, and it was colder than usual that spring in the Yukon. That night was frigid and our tent was covered with rime, inside and out, but we were warm and happy. The next morning's first chore was to carefully scrape the inside rime off with spoons onto a cloth which we emptied outside, keeping tent as dry as possible. It was cloudy, visibility less than a hundred feet, causing a forced rest day which I cherished and the others needed. For part of the day we scrunched into Dave and Paul's tent to play cards, help them reduce their excess weight in food and contemplate questions from "The Question Book," questions like "How many lovers have you had and would you rather have had more or less?" and "On a scale of 1–10, 1 being suffering, hardship and great accomplishment, 10 being comfort, peace of mind and no accomplishment, where would you like to be and where would you describe yourself right now?"

My journal of the 28th reads:

> I am in good company. The route up here went through some of the most spectacular, beautiful snow/icescape I've ever seen. We could see Logan and St. Elias, and I thought of my wonderful friend Stelling and of his great endeavor on Logan and of how happy he would be to be here doing this. I was amazed at the mass of Logan. Strange to think of the ocean just on the other side of St. Elias, from here in this vast, mini-Antarctic ice cap landscape....The basics—a tomato/basil soup last night was as enjoyable a meal as I have ever had. We both said so. A room with a view. A dry, warm tent. Company you can enjoy and depend on. A warm bed in the night with Lady J. Hot tea with sugar. Hot coffee.....My hands are cracked and painful. Otherwise, I feel fine.....I feel so connected in this isolated place. The effort required to be here and the lack of civilization's demands and complexities and horrors, allows the self to see, appreciate and embrace the reality, that by itself the self has no self that can be defined.

As I said, the best thing about climbing is the places it gets you to.

And we wanted to be on top of Steele. Accordingly, on the morning of April 29th we got a leisurely and late start in the unavailing hope that temperatures would rise with the sun. We left Camp Four at 9:45 in the morning, Dave and Paul about 20 minutes ahead. Bitter cold with high winds. Clear. I put chemical hand warmer packets in each mitten, and, as with my extra rest day, they made all the difference. In climbing as elsewhere, technology, despite its tendency to degrade the natural world and create two new problems for each old one solved, is useful. I don't think my hands would have survived the climb without the warm packets. For the first two hours we were on skis, moving up a circuitous route around crevasses on hard, wind blown snow over ice and sastrugi runnels. I was much stronger and warmer than expected, and, as a result, my confidence, enjoyment and awareness of the day were at full power. We took a break around noon, changing tools from skis and poles to crampons and ice ax and one ski pole. We drank some water and ate. The summit of Steele was a long, steep, wind scoured snow slope above.

With Lady J in the lead we began the last push. It was cold but bearable. Lady J kept a consistent pace, expecting, she later said, the rope to come taut as I dropped back. But I have probably never had a better or stronger day in the mountains and was able to maintain her pace. I quickly focused on breathing and on being in the moment of placing each cramponed foot exactly right while moving ice ax and ski pole up in rhythm. Breath and rhythm. Slow and steady. Step. Step. Conscious breathing is an ancient practice of all people who carry loads in high places. On this occasion it produced a lovely state of disposition, one of the best I've ever known in climbing. If there is a transcendent mountain state of mind, that was it. I moved through my own efforts and the outside elements with confidence and what can only be described as joy, a fitting compensation for how one lives one's life. Summit day was for me the easiest and most graceful period of the entire climb. After an hour and a half of sustained and very enjoyable climbing we were at the base of the summit pyramid. Dave and Paul met us as they descended, suggesting that we put everything on because of the fierce wind on top. "It's really cold Dave emphasized. (We later estimated that it was minus 20 degrees Fahrenheit with 60 mph winds, and all three of them agreed it was colder than on Mt. Logan two years before and 3000 feet higher.

It was among the coldest summits any of us had ever experienced.)

We congratulated Dave and Paul and continued up as they descended. There were a few technical moves on the last, steep and icy section, but we moved efficiently together and suddenly Lady J vanished onto the summit block above. I came over the top to be greeted by a powerful wind and the brightest of smiles. The top of Mt. Steele that day was as cold as the heart of a man who takes no prisoners. Lady J's smile was as warm as a summer sun. She gave me a kiss and a hug and a few just-right words. She took a photo of me and insisted we didn't need one of her. But we did need to get off the summit. After approximately 20 seconds on top we did just that, descending quickly to a lower elevation where the winds were less robust and dangerous. We laughed. I was supremely happy. An hour later we got back to the skis and took a break for food and fluid before returning to camp. We talked about the fine day and about a goal accomplished. We spoke about Lady J's desire to climb Lucania, which she and Dave and Paul did four days later in a ten hour push. I opted out because I could not have kept their pace for ten hours and to move slower would have jeopardized success. Lady J will have to tell you about that climb, and perhaps she will sometime. There will be other goals and other days for both of us, but climbing Steele with Lady J gave me, at least for a time, the priceless gifts that can't be measured or bought or bargained for ... a peaceful heart and a satisfied mind and the unbelievably good feeling of a body well used and tired in the good way that brings health and strength to be used in that same good way another day.

The author on the summit of Mt. Steele   *photo Jeannie Wall*

CHAPTER EIGHT

The Spirits of Kennedy

AT ABOUT 11,000 FEET, something didn't fit. An object in the jumble
of ice fall, serac, crevasse, glacier and snow about half a mile away
seemed disharmonious with this natural arctic landscape of granite
and perpetual winter. In the interests of weight, I'd left my binoculars
in base camp, nearly 5000 feet lower. My partner Jeannie Wall and I
took a break from our labors of the past several hours, hauling a sled
and heavy packs up the Cathedral Glacier on the south flank of Mt.
Kennedy in Canada's Yukon. That morning we left our skis at 9500 feet
and continued upward using crampons and ski poles. The glacial hours
passed slowly. We gained hard-earned altitude through a convoluted
icefall, over and around but, fortunately, not into any of the countless
hidden and obvious crevasses. It was our third day of earnest, continuous
drudgery since being dropped off by plane on the glacier at 6400 feet.
Any plausible excuse for a break—like stopping to determine if a dark
slice in the ice was the tricky shadow of a crack or an object that shouldn't
be there—was welcome. We rested and squinted, lamenting the decision
to leave binoculars behind, and finally agreed it had to be a vertical crack
in the face of an ice block, eyes tricking minds or minds deceiving eyes.
Though something about it didn't rest well in the back of my mind and
the core of my instincts, we let it go and continued.

Moving up is the job and the joy at hand. In climbing as in the rest
of life it is always upwards until something significant happens—the
summit, the retreat, the defeat, the accident, the end of time, the sudden

remembrance of other things to do. The only meaningful movement is personal, accomplished in small increments, both inward and out, one step, one move, one small understanding at a time. Most moves are slow and arduously made. Few are individually remembered. It is the entire mountain, the whole life that is momentous. One climbs not because the climb is obviously there, but because those personal understandings hidden within the process of the climb are to be found nowhere else, meaningful only to the individual who gains them. Summits come and go and sometimes do not come at all, but the personal knowledge, mind tricks and all, remains. As Maurice Herzog so famously put it, "There is an Annapurna in the life of every man." If there is a more rational rationale for climbing I have not seen it. In addition, the process is great fun, outrageously interesting, all the exercise you need, and more often than not carried out in some of the loveliest and wildest environments on earth. If you're lucky, as I am, you get to climb with people as untamed and lovely as the environment.

An hour later we joined the two fastest members of our party, Paul Barry and Dave Hart, at high camp, 11,700. They had camped higher than us the previous night, carrying all their food and gear in one load. The rest of us had to ferry our burdens. I mean, Paul and Dave are extremely strong in the mountains, as strong as draft horses, and we nicknamed them 'Clyde' and 'Dale.' They had already dug platforms and wind walls in the snow and set up tents and were slumbering after their exertions. We woke them and they were surprised we had made it so quickly. Jeannie and I had moved up 3000 feet over about four miles with heavy loads through tricky if technically easy terrain in five hours. I felt strong. Jeannie is a Czarina of endurance endeavor and the winner of the 2002 American Birkebeiner ski race, is always strong. The weather was excellent for the Yukon in May, sunny and clear and around 25 degrees Fahrenheit in the middle of the day. Temperatures plummet to below zero when the sun gets low in late afternoon.

We quickly dug a platform and wind walls and set up our tent and began the interminable cold-weather climber's chore of melting snow for water, hot drinks, and food. The three other members of our party,

Canadians Greg Jacob and Karen Herzenberg and the American Andy Evans, were three hours behind. By evening they had arrived and the seven of us had fashioned a three-tiered camp on the uneven glacier: three tents for sleeping and a fourth that Greg, Karen and Andy used for cooking and we all used for social gatherings.

Ours was an ambitious and accomplished group of climbers. My six climbing mates were using this outing as training for bigger things. First Mt. Kennedy (13,860 feet) Mt. Alverstone (14,500 feet) and Mt. Hubbard (14,950 feet). Then Jeannie, Dave, Paul and Greg will fly to King Peak (16,900 feet) and attempt a second ascent of the southwest ridge, a route that had turned Jeannie, Paul and Dave back the year before. Andy and Karen intend to climb the east ridge of Mt. Logan (19,400 feet), the second highest peak in North America. My own modest objective is simply to climb Kennedy in good style, savor the experience, and pay homage to and be reminded of John (for whom the mountain is named) and Bobby Kennedy and to their time in American history. The Kennedys' intelligence and vision offered more promise and hope for a better world and America than I have perceived since their time, and when the opportunity came my way to climb Kennedy I was drawn to it.

My fate of late finds me often climbing with partners 20 to 30 years younger, and, naturally, Mt. Kennedy has a different resonance for them than for me. Politically, and, therefore, socially, this group covers the entire spectrum, with me at the left edge and Paul at, and sometimes over, the right. I am the only one for whom Mt. Kennedy has a living, or at least lived, instead of only historical significance. Such is the fortunate destiny of one who continues to climb when many of my contemporaries do not, and who is lucky enough to have climbing friends not even born on November 22, 1963 who tolerate the intolerable foibles of one who marks the beginning of the war on America's soul, survival and freedoms from that date, almost 40 years before September 11, 2001.

America's 60s were a time of expansion and growth, personal and social change, and Cultural Revolution, when social protest and personal experimentation took to the streets, forests, deserts, rivers, rock walls, and mountains of America. It was a time when the dominant mood of the nation was one of hope and promise, not fear and suspicion. I am of that time, and the action of the climb reinvigorates my hope that such a mood can return to our present suspicious and fearful nation.

The civil rights movement was legitimized by the Kennedys' bold and creative perception of America's possibilities, and that perception and imagination found its way into the spirit of American mountaineering. The Kennedys were leaders, not CEOs or members of the Board of Directors. In early 1963 the first Americans climbed Everest by the South Col route, closely followed by Willi Unsoeld and Tom Hornbein's courageous and inspired ascent of the West Face, certainly among the most demanding and committing climbs in history. In Yosemite Warren Harding, Royal Robbins, Chuck Pratt, Yvon Chouinard, Tom Frost, Frank Sacherer, T.M. Herbert and a congregation of lesser known rock jocks put up bold and brilliant routes on the biggest rock walls that had yet been climbed. In the process of imagining, learning and developing the technology and techniques to climb the ramparts of America's most beautiful valley they raised the standards and changed the possibilities for climbing and climbers everywhere. These climbs were very much in the spirit and attitude of the Kennedys and their time. Though they and their vision were shot down in mid-stride by a couple of dirty little cowards the Kennedy legacy lives on (much as it galls certain elements of conservative American society and politics). Climbing Mt. Kennedy was in some small part paying my respect to them and their legacy and to some members of the family whom I consider friends. But the primary reason was to experience and enjoy a superb climb within my capabilities with good friends in a truly wild environment, and, in the process, understand something more of myself and my friends. Experience. Enjoyment. New knowledge. Fresh understanding. Reasons and rewards enough for doing anything.

If this be part nostalgia for the spirit of a vibrant time as much as motivation for a lovely climb, it is nostalgia not without hope for a return of the lost spirits of generosity, intelligence and candor in national affairs. The nation could use the kind of bluntness Bobby Kennedy showed when he said, "People are sick of politicians. And they are looking for ... just an honest man." Yes, the nation could always use an honest man.

Fourteen months after John Kennedy's death on November 22, 1963, the Canadian Government named the highest unclimbed peak in North America after him. Bradford Washburn described it as a "magnificent Matterhorn-like mountain." In March 1965 it was climbed for the first time by an eight man party, including Jim Whitaker, the first American up Everest, and by then U.S. Senator Robert F. "Bobby" Kennedy. Within certain climbing circles I have heard the story that Bobby Kennedy was helicoptered to 13,200 on the mountain and was then roped up and hauled up the rest of the climb. This is not true, and, since the accurate account of the ascent is readily available in the climbing literature, one can only conclude that this mean-spirited rumor has been nurtured by some combination of political/social/philosophical enemies of the Kennedys, standard bearers for the mystique of machismo mountaineering which Gary Snyder has described as "the hostile, jock Occidental mind-set that thought to climb a mountain was to conquer it," and those somehow threatened by the reality that even an inexperienced, out of shape Senator from Washington, D.C. can get up a good climb if he puts his mind and spirit and will in order.

In fact, Kennedy was helicoptered to 8700 feet on the Cathedral Glacier, climbed to 11,000 feet the following day and a day later reached the summit in a five hour push. Washburn wrote of this climb, "Although this ascent via Cathedral Glacier does not involve any technical problems of consequence, Mount Kennedy is a superb peak and the view from its summit is one of the finest in the Yukon.... The most extraordinary aspect of the climb of March 1965 was the fact that Senator Kennedy made the round trip to the summit of Mount Kennedy from Washington, D.C. in barely 5 days—an incredible tour de force and a remarkable accomplishment for someone who had never climbed before."

Bobby Kennedy made a first ascent of the highest unclimbed peak in North America and he left an unidentified "memento" of his dead brother in the summit snows. One can imagine with what affection and emotion Bobby left that memento, and one wonders about his novice climber's experience and enjoyment and what new knowledge and fresh understanding came to him on the slopes of ice and snow of Mt. Kennedy. Not every climber believes in spirits, but for those who do the spirits of Mt. Kennedy include Bobby's fine effort and achievement, John's memento, their legacy to America (probably best given voice at that time by the perseverance and articulate, valuable work in the U.S. Senate of Ted Kennedy and the eloquent, vital and effective environmental activism of Bobby Kennedy Jr.) and the significance to American and world history of the lives and deaths of those two good men.

Their lives, like all those with the ambitious freedoms to indulge in such consequential behavior as high level politics or cold weather climbing, were the stuff of extraordinary beauty and tragedy, good fortune and star-crossed adversity, intelligent sophistication and primordial ambition, inspired (and inspiring) achievement and humbling limitations. In the Yukon these indulgences take place in dazzling surroundings—endless glaciated valleys, huge ice falls, wild granite peaks stretching as far as the eye can see, filled with all the subtle changing blue/green/black/white colors of snow and ice and rock and devoid of human mark except, in our case, the bit left by a few climbers. The stark white view in all directions from our camp is reason and rewards enough for the efforts that got us there. The scenery, perspective and understanding that go with it are equal to any other, including those from the Oval Office of the White House; and I cannot help but be curious about what White House thoughts came to Bobby Kennedy on the Cathedral Glacier and on the summit slope of Mt. Kennedy.

The front door of our tent opened to the south on a spectacular arctic mountain vista. In the distance, Alaska's Mt. Fairweather loomed above everything to the southwest. Closer by, the beautiful, steep lines of The Weisshorn dominated the view to the southeast, but we zipped the door shut as the temperature dropped, retreating into the comfort of our tent cocoon, the thinnest of modern technological mountain shelters. 1/16th of an inch is slender separation from the realities of Yukon weather, including the wind storm from hell and temperatures that could turn the warmest blood to ice. In most life situations, 1/16th of an inch margin is sufficient for all but the unexpected. But the unexpected assassin—the bullet from nowhere, the momentary lapse in judgment, the wrong information, stupidity, ambition without integrity or tempering, confidence without humility, the fiercest storm, the avalanche, the icefall collapse, the broken crampon on the crux move, the crevasse, the fall—is always unexpected.

Inside our thin but sturdy tent manufactured in Asia by people paid a barely subsistence wage, we slept in bags made of down plucked from many geese designed to keep a human body warm at minus 20 degrees Fahrenheit, on pads made of unpronounceable substances originating in the oils of Saudi Arabia that insulate against ice, after ingesting a delicious dinner of Thai cuisine cooked on a Swedish stove the size of a fist, followed by tea grown in India and Hob Nobs cookies made in Great Britain. A SAT phone connected members of our party with girl friends in Anchorage, wives in Calgary, mothers (on Mother's Day) in Ontario and Pennsylvania and Wisconsin, weathermen in Yakitat, our pilot in Chitna and even a party of climbers with another SAT phone on Mt. Logan. We are modern climbers, up-to-the-minute people of the world. Even in the remote Yukon, we are connected to, citizens of, dependent on, and responsible to and for all the other humans, creatures and environments that comprise the world community. Self-sufficiency as a personal quality goal is, of course, admirable and necessary and no climber would get very far without it; but as an absolute value it is an illusion. It does not exist. Like isolationism as a national policy, it is a self-serving hall of creed's (and greed's) mirrors benefiting few at the expense of many.

We slept the sleep of those who have pushed hard with heavy loads for three consecutive days. A day of rest was in order, but the weather was beautiful: clear skies and no wind early on the morning of May 8. In the Yukon it is an indulgence to sit out a day of good weather, and we did not. We were up and moving by 9 a.m. toward the summit of Mt. Kennedy.

From my journal of May 8, 2002:

Camp at 11,700. Evening. Full of ravioli and hot chocolate. The end of one of my all time best days in the mountains. We climbed Mt. Kennedy today in excellent time and in perfect weather. Jeannie and I on one rope, Paul and Dave on another. The Canadians stayed here and made a ferry from the cache at 10,700. I was able to keep pace pretty well, but the boys are faster and reached the summit about 20 minutes before us. The final summit ridge is a true snow arête with long drops off each side and a tricky technical section in the middle on hard ice. The views from the summit in every direction are wonderful— Steele, Lucania, Logan, St. Elias, Alverstone, Fairweather and, of course, the ocean. We took photos and hung out for 20 minutes and came down. I said, 'Here's to John and Bobby' while we were on the summit, but either the reference missed my mates or they were not of a mind to honor the Kennedys. I had some good thoughts of Bobby Kennedy, both of his climbing the peak and of his political life and, of course, his family, particularly my friend, Chris, one of his sons, whom I think of often but have not seen in years. We went up and back in five and a half hours, and I am extremely tired. After four days of carrying loads and keeping up with Jeannie I am depleted.

At the summit I was once again reminded that extraordinary beauty and tragedy, good fortune and star-crossed adversity move together in the mountains, one never very far from the other. We were thrilled to see Mt. Steele, which the four of us had climbed two years earlier, a fine experience. The Kennedy Glacier and The Great Shelf spread out below us like two frozen lakes in the mountains of wonder. We also saw human tracks topping out from the Northeast ridge. In 1965 Washburn had written of this route, "The first ascent of its 6,000 foot northeast ridge from the Lowell Glacier will rank as a first-class granite-and-ice climb—one of Canada's top remaining mountaineering challenges." Jack Tackle called it "the most beautiful route in the world." These tracks had been left ten months earlier and no one else had been up Kennedy since, and Paul and Dave knew the story, but had not mentioned it until we saw the tracks: The Americans Andy Selters and Bill Pilling had climbed the northeast ridge in good style. They descended the route we had just climbed and camped near where our high camp was located, intending to climb Alverstone before descending to the lower Cathedral Glacier to be picked up by plane. But a six day storm pinned them down, causing them to run out of food and fuel without climbing Alverstone. (Such are the vagaries of Yukon weather that ten months and numerous storms will not erase tracks at 13,000 feet while making movement impossible at 11,000.) After the storm, their pilot, Kurt Gloyer, flew into their agreed pickup spot and when he didn't see them continued up the glacier in his Cessna 185 searching for them. When Andy and Bill heard the plane they stamped the message FOOD and FUEL in the snow, to describe their predicament. Though that part of the glacier is neither flat nor particularly smooth, Gloyer decided to land and rescue the climbers rather than making another trip, dropping them food and fuel and letting them descend to the lower glacier. The landing went okay, but the Cessna lacked the power necessary to take off at that altitude with that load from that terrain. The doomed takeoff was bumpy and the plane jumped over a few crevasses before the prop and skis plowed into a snow ridge and broke off. The plane skidded and then crashed into the last crevasse in the series. Gloyer was killed and Selters and Pilling were seriously injured. Two accomplished climbers had safely climbed "the most beautiful route in the world" in good style. Their endeavor had been a success, but in the end they were ambushed by unexpected tragedy. I am reminded of the eloquent observation of James Salter which could apply to the adventurous lives of a couple of climbers, the privileged lives of Bobby and John Kennedy, and to you and me and everyone we know and love: "We are each of us an eventual tragedy."

Jeannie and I later determined that the disharmonious object we had viewed in the ice fall the day before was, in fact, the Cessna's broken prop frozen in place. Our eyes had not deceived us, but our minds, lacking knowledge of the wreck, could not conceive that an airplane propeller would be sticking up in a high mountain glacier of the Yukon. We could not believe the truth of our own eyes, an object lesson about the human condition and the workings of the mind. When the high mast ships of the Portuguese/Spanish explorer/sailor Magellan first appeared off the eastern coast of southern South America in 1520, it is said that the Patagones (Big Feet, the name Magellan gave to the indigenous people because of the size of their feet and their ability to run long distances, and from which the region Patagonia derives its name) did not believe the truth of their eyes and did not see the ships because they had never seen a ship before. Because they could not imagine the unimaginable, they were unable to see the earliest seeds of their destruction. The indigenous Patagones are an extinct people now, and it is not too much to imagine that had they believed the integrity of their own eyes and dealt with Magellan as the threat to their lives and way of living he was, they might have insured their survival. Certainly they would have prolonged it.

It takes the leap of imagination, the innocence of youth and the courage of trust to believe the honesty of one's own eyes and other senses. We had easily succeeded in the modest if beautiful endeavor of climbing Mt. Kennedy. On the summit we were happy and satisfied with our efforts. Our climb had been successful and rewarding by all the inner and outer measures of a climb. It was only later that I came to ponder the spirits of Kennedy and the new realization that we had been able to ignore the evidence of our own eyes, to look at something that our eyes told us did not belong there and to convince our minds that it was something it was not. It was another of those personal understandings that are to be found nowhere else. In all the mountains and valleys of life it is necessary to trust our eyes and instincts and to follow their leads to understanding instead of stopping at the first rest stop of self-delusion. To take the easy path of ignoring them is dangerous and slothful and, in the end, self-defeating. It is not inconceivable that the day might come when having the imagination to trust one's own eyes and senses, even in a completely foreign context and frame of reference, could be the difference between an eventual tragedy and the gift of a new understanding. In this instance, no harm came to us for mistaking a part of a plane wreck for a crack in the ice, but it is that potential in all of us to seek the easy understanding, even if it is false, that falsely serves the world and our selves.

We climb to seek understandings of what we demand of ourselves as climbers and what the world demands of us as citizens. Bobby Kennedy described them thus:

> *This world demands the qualities of youth; not a time of life but a state of mind, a temper of will, a quality of imagination, a predominance of courage over timidity, of the appetite for adventure over the love of ease.*

Thanks John. Thanks Bobby. May they who spurned the love of ease rest in peace.

Yosemite   *from a 19th-century engraving by Thomas Moran*

CHAPTER NINE

You Can't Go Home Again

Most often we think of the natural world as an economic resource, or as a place of recreation after a wearisome period of work, or as something of passing interest for its beauty on an autumn day when the radiant colors of the oak and maple leaves give us a moment of joy. All these attitudes are quite legitimate, yet in them all there is what might be called a certain trivializing attitude. If we were truly moved by the beauty of the world about us, we would honor the earth in a profound way. We would understand immediately and turn away with a certain horror from all those activities that violate the integrity of the planet.

That we have not done so reveals that a disturbance exists at a more basic level of consciousness and on a greater order of magnitude than we dare to admit to ourselves or even think about. This unprecedented pathology is not merely in those more immediate forms of economic activity that have done such damage; it is even more deeply imbedded in our cultural traditions, in our religious traditions, in our very language, in our entire value system.
—Thomas Berry

JUST BEFORE HIS UNTIMELY DEATH from tubercular meningitis American novelist Thomas Wolfe finished his last work, "You Can't Go Home Again," about a writer who has written a successful novel about his home town. When he returns to his town the writer finds its citizens full of hatred, resentment, rejection and scorn towards him for what he has revealed to the world and to themselves about themselves. In response, the writer becomes a wanderer in search of a home to replace the one to which he cannot return. The novel, a great one in my opinion, is required reading for the disaffected of America. The phrase "You can't go home again," has become part of the lexicon of cliché (or wisdom, depending), such as "You can't go to the same party twice," and "You can't step in the same river twice," by which we orient ourselves and understand a hurriedly changing world.

That you can't go home again is a primordial tragedy, one not to be confused with foolish and futile, though sometimes enjoyable efforts to reclaim the past. Whether this elemental disaster is part of the human condition or unique to the past hundred years is a useful query. So is whether the spirit of reclaiming the past is mournful or celebratory. Both are valuable questions for another time and place; but they are entirely different matters.

Such thoughts have been wandering more than usual through my disaffected brain since this past May (2004) when I took my first climbing trip to Yosemite Valley in several years. I first arrived in the Yosemite climbing scene in the spring of 1968, and spent a considerable amount of time there for the next six or seven years. I missed by a few years the height of the golden years of Yosemite climbing, but I certainly inhaled deeply of its mellow yellow years. I climbed hard and thoroughly enjoyed what was (and is) some of the best rock climbing on earth. I found a suitable niche and immersed myself in what was (and is) the free-form, eclectic, high-energy, social experiment revolving around that scene. It was a great time of life for many reasons, among them the irreplaceable good fortune of being able to live for long periods of time in the midst of the beauty of the Yosemite Valley, to climb each day with the finest of climbing partners and comrades, and to return at night to the simple and Spartan existence (some would say decadence) that characterized climbers' lives in Camp 4. It was a paradise of sorts for disaffected Americans who had wandered or been driven into climbing, populated by few who ever made it into the mainstream. Even those who would later become wealthy and well known in American society have a tenuous hold in the mainstream.

If we were truly moved by the beauty of the world about us, we would honor the earth in a profound way. We would understand immediately and turn away with a certain horror from all those activities that violate the integrity of the planet.

If we are not truly moved by the unrivaled beauty of the Yosemite, then what possible means do we have to honor the earth? More, if we are not truly moved, what are we, truly?

That we (Homo sapiens) embrace rather than turn away in horror from those activities that violate the integrity of the earth is self-evident.

If we were truly moved we would understand immediately, but we aren't and we don't; and our profound confusion, ignorance and stupidity are as clear in Yosemite as the air of California is not. The Yosemite I found last spring is a growing monument to what Berry terms a trivializing attitude mankind has towards the integrity of the planet. As a species, we suffer from a pathology not shared by any other creature on earth. It affects all the creatures and all the places of the earth, the formerly inspirational ones like Yosemite as well as the always corrupting ones like the freeways of Los Angeles, the stale waters of Lake Powell, the toxic brew of the Berkley Pit of Butte, Montana, the air of Mexico City, the clear cut logging wounds of Oregon and Washington and British Columbia and Brazil and Costa Rica and elsewhere and the radiated grounds of Hanford, Washington, among others.

On a cloudless California mid-May late afternoon we drove into Yosemite Valley from Crane Flat, as we had done so often in other times. I had not climbed in Yosemite for some 15 years, and the last time was with Galen Rowell. On that occasion, we had been unable to secure a place to camp in the valley, and, along with Galen's wife and partner, Barbara Cushman Rowell, we had stayed in Mariposa, commuting each day up to the valley to climb. In my enthusiasm to climb, I hadn't given adequate thought to the significance of a Yosemite Valley with no room for another camp site. That had never been my experience. Each morning we drove up from Mariposa, climbed, and returned in the evening. The climbing was great and to ride in an automobile driven by Galen was a completely absorbing adventure that made it difficult to notice anything beyond the next curve in the road. Being a passenger of Galen's usually felt like being on lead at the limit of your abilities with the last protection 25 feet below your feet, except you didn't get to make the moves. Galen did. That is, Galen's passengers didn't tend to notice scenery, much less landscape and environmental subtleties. For whatever reasons, I didn't really see Yosemite on that trip.

On this last trip, as my friend Jeannie and I drove down into the valley on the Crane Flat road, my excitement to be again in one of my favorite places was tempered with nostalgic memories of Galen and Barbara, who were killed two years ago, and colored with less melancholy reminiscences of people, climbs and events of another time. The awareness that you can't go home again makes that home more poignant and, perhaps, meaningful in the present moment. Both Jeannie and I had climbed in Yosemite but never together, and we were pleased enough to arrive in "the valley" that we sloughed off our residual irritation and frustration with the congestion, traffic, exhaust fumes, haze and inattentive driving practices of the tourists encountered along Highway 49 as it passes through the chic and celebrated towns that serve as monuments and trendy consumer outlets to California's gold mining history—Coloma, Placerville, El Dorado, Sutter Creek, Mokulumne Hill, Angels Camp and Chinese Camp. Naturally, our annoyance with California crowds was in no way alleviated by the awareness that we were as complicit as any, a part of the crowd, jockeying for position in pursuit of our own missions of overriding importance, emitting our share of carbon dioxide and angst to the stew of global warming air with each mile we drove. Irony should be a required subject in the public education of every citizen.

On both sides of the road the signs of the devastating fires of a few years ago were evident, as were the regenerative powers of nature. The blackened husks of fir and pine and cedar, standing and fallen, were a stark contrast to the carpet of green rising from the ashes of yesterday's infernos. Forest fires are as natural and necessary as the turning of the seasons. That we choose to fight rather than adapt to them is one of many symptoms of the pathology to which Berry refers. The green that springs from fire's ash is the greenest of them all.

Yosemite classic climbing areas appeared: Reed's Pinnacle above the road, the Cookie somewhere below, the Rostrum across the lower canyon, and then after Highway 120 meets the valley floor, the main Yosemite rock features come into view, the Cathedral Rocks, Sentinel, El Capitan, Half Dome. There is no sight quite like it in the world I know. A rock climber could spend several lives there without exploring it all, and some climbers have done and are doing just that. More than 130 years ago John Muir described Yosemite:

> *The most extravagant description I might give of this view to any one who has not seen similar landscapes with his own eyes would not so much as hint its grandeur and the spiritual glow that covered it ... The level bottom seemed to be dressed like a garden—sunny meadows here and there, and groves of pine and oak; the river of Mercy sweeping in majesty through the midst of them and flashing back the sunbeams. The great Tissiack, or Half-Dome, rising at the upper end of the valley to a height of nearly a mile, is nobly proportioned and life-like, the most impressive of all the rocks, holding the eye in devout admiration, calling it back again and again from falls and meadows, or even the mountains beyond,—marvelous cliffs, marvelous in sheer dizzy depth and sculpture, types of endurance. Thousands of years have they stood in the sky exposed to rain, snow, frost, earthquake and avalanche, yet they still wear the bloom of youth.*

"... the spiritual glow that covered it."
"... the bloom of youth."

How things change. Signs of Yosemite's transformation during the past 30 years are inescapable and clear. Tens of thousands of years of rain, snow, frost, earthquake and avalanche, to say nothing of hundreds of years of the Ahwahnee Indians burning the valley floor from time to time to regenerate it, changed Yosemite Valley far less than a hundred and fifty years of the trivializing attitude of modern man. John Muir would have a hard time recognizing Yosemite today. Only a National Park Service booster or a flack for Yosemite concessionaires would be crass and inexact enough to describe Yosemite as covered in a spiritual glow or exhibiting the bloom of youth. Muir, of course, was neither mindless booster nor servile flack; but the Yosemite experience which touched Muir so deeply and which he described so movingly and extravagantly is no longer available to modern man. And the sad if salient reality is that Muir, like the rest of us, inadvertently (at least for most of us) contributed to Yosemite's demise, and we continue to do so.

Yosemite is a microcosm/metaphor for life on earth.

The first and most obvious thing one notices on the valley floor of Yosemite after a several year absence, the river of Mercy continuing to run through its core, is the traffic. Automobiles controlled by several wildly different pilot systems—auto, agro, bozo, spaceo, mano-a-mano, retro, macho, dumbo and weirdo—clog the one road, stopping unexpectedly whenever a distraction short circuits the pilot system. It is California, after all, where automobiles rule, and ours contributes its fair share to the congestion and smog of the golden state, diluting clarity of vision, filling lungs with toxins. This black carbon smog is not limited to California, of course, nor is its underlying cause of overpopulation of the planet. According to Veerabhadran Ramanathan of the Scripps Institution of Oceanography in La Jolla, a brown cloud of dust, pollution and chemicals is absorbing solar radiation and scattering sunlight before it reaches earth. Nowhere is this more evident than in the Sierra Nevada of California, including Yosemite, which produces its own share of pollution but is also downwind from the air pollution capital of California, Los Angeles. The clarity of Yosemite's once pristine air and vistas are gone, a fact and metaphor of modern life. A dirty haze covers Yosemite, some of it caused not by automobiles but by controlled burns still smoldering and pumping smoke into the already corrupted air. The photos of Ansel Adams are images from another world. Even he couldn't take those wonderful photographs now. A sign at Fern Springs warns against drinking the water. We used to fill all our water bottles at

Fern Springs, considering it the best drinking water in the valley. So far as I know, no one in our circles ever got sick from Fern Springs water, but the sign is there for a reason and I believe it.

Our friend Helen has a camp site for us, but she has not yet checked in via cell phone and we do not know where to go and have some spare time. We drive around the valley in bumper to bumper traffic to Camp 4. I am curious about my old haunt. A few years ago Camp 4 was slated to be shut down and turned into housing. The climbing community, led by Tom Frost and Dick Duane, reacted and fought and lobbied and sued and managed to give Camp 4 Federal Historical status. As a result it is still a walk-in camp for Yosemite climbers, and all climbers are pleased. The parking area is packed, but we find a place and take a sentimental lap around Camp 4. Most of the citizens of Camp 4 are 30 to 40 years my junior and easily recognizable as climber dirtbags for a day or a season or three seasons or a lifetime, depending. Neither of us knows any of them. One gray haired fellow with the look of many hard moves and uncomfortable bivouacs is a couple decades older than anyone around him. He looks vaguely familiar but I cannot place him. We exchange nods and smiles of recognition and the kinship of age but do not speak. We watch a young lad practicing with astonishing skill on a slack line hung between two trees. Groups of climbers are telling climbing stories, complete with acting out the moves of the crux. Others are bouldering. A few parties are already in progress. A couple is setting up their tent. There are lots of tents. There are more men than women, and the boys are hanging around every camp with girls. A forlorn looking climber with still taped hands is sitting in a chair beside his pack and rope drinking a beer, staring at without seeing a point in the distance. Even after 30 years, many aspects of Camp 4 are familiar, easily recognizable, almost like going home.

Barely is enough, but almost doesn't count.

Other aspects, much like the black carbon smog substituting for air in California, are overridingly unrecognizable. The ground of Camp 4 has been trodden into a lifeless hardpan that is the antithesis of spiritual glow or the bloom of youth. It obviously would be and has been and will be again a mud bog in a hard rain. Lots of tents, lots of people, not much room between them. I estimate that 10 times more climbers inhabit Camp 4 now than in the '60s and '70s. It is an overcrowded if logical extension of the rest of Yosemite, but, unless we connect with Helen, it is the only available camping in the valley. I told Jeannie that even if we have to drive to Wawona or Mariposa each night, I do not want to stay in Camp 4. She agrees. Fortunately, when we get back to the car there is a message from Helen with directions to a camp site among the Winnebagos, generators and the rollout Astroturf patios under fold up awnings. And, in the interest of full disclosure, we were happy to have it. We set up camp, cooked dinner, ate, talked into the night and slept in our tents in comfort. A bear wandered through camp in the night looking for the one camper there will always be who neglects to put food in the steel bear proof boxes abundantly scattered throughout the valley. Bear found no such neglect in our neighborhood that night, but he left a large pile of bear shit next to one of the tents just to say hello.

The next morning, after coffee and muffins in the chill haze, we went to the base of El Capitan for the day's projects. There were scant places to park along the road near El Cap, but we found one and had soon made the short hike up to the rock. Just as we arrived at the base we encountered a climbing acquaintance of Helen's helping his partner down the path. His partner had (obviously) badly broken his ankle in a fall several hundred feet up the Salathe Wall, and they had spent the past few hours getting down. We dropped our packs and spent the next 45 minutes helping carry the wounded rock warrior to their car. We were tired and our backs were sore by the time we finally got back to the rock and racked up and ready to climb. We began with the classic La Cosita, right, which was, as always, hard, strenuous, beautiful and very, very polished from thousands of ascents. The fine granite of Yosemite's most trafficked free climbs is worn as smooth by hands and feet and the placement of gear as glaciers and rivers have polished rock throughout the Sierra Nevada. But the slippery cracks of Yosemite climbing were polished in far less time than it took the glaciers and rivers.

At the end of the day I was belaying Helen as she struggled with the off width moves at the top of Sacherer Cracker. The sun was behind El Cap and it was cold. Jeannie suddenly said, "Dick, don't look now, but there's a bear about ten feet behind you." Sure enough, there he was, a large, somehow unhealthy and goofy looking bear scoping out our packs for food content. Since I was occupied and Helen did not want my attention distracted, even by bears, I told Jeannie to throw rocks at him but not to hit him. She did and bear scampered away a few yards. She threw some more stones and bear vanished only to appear a few minutes later, waiting to make his move. Jeannie threw rocks and shouted, "Go away, bear." I belayed and shivered. Helen, among the coolest, quietest climbers on a hard lead I've ever known, silently struggled and sweated. Bear was patient, persistent and wary, but he kept appearing every few minutes until, shortly before we left, he vanished as quietly as he had appeared. Tommy Caldwell and partner walked by, coming down from fixing some pitches on the Dihedral. I recognized Caldwell from magazine photos and we talked about the bear and the problem of bears at the base of El Cap. They left. I thought of his famous Asian mis-adventure and of the ultimate climber's nightmare of being shot at while on a wall, a prospect which puts a certain perspective on the 'problem' of bears, even grizzly bears. Give me a grizzly with his natural disposition and hunger and turf over the lunacy of a fundamentalist (not all of them Islamic) with (or even without) a weapon, any day.

Grizzly bears were once plentiful in California, and the grizzly (*Ursus arctos horribilis*) is on the state flag. The Golden Bears of California are named for the grizzly. However, as a difficult neighbor for the anthropocentric and those unable, unwilling or too ignorant to honor the earth in a profound way, the grizzly was exterminated from California by 1922. The last grizzly known to have been killed in Yosemite was in 1895. The black bear (*Ursus americanus*), more amenable to human encroachment upon the land, has remained. For many years' black bear/human encounters and conflicts, though not unknown, were manageable, in some part because the Yosemite garbage dump provided a substitute for the reduced food supply in the bears' shrinking natural habitat. Then in the late 1960s the dump was shut down and

Yosemite's garbage was trucked out of the valley. The bears of Yosemite lost the food source to which they had become habituated. Naturally, as they had when their first and natural source of food was cut off, they went to the next best option: the plethora of food items brought into Yosemite by hikers, climbers, back packers, campers and drive-through gawkers, easily gathered in many forms and wrappings on camp tables and in tents, backpacks, cars, vans, ice coolers, garbage cans, haul bags, and, in a few rare and particularly pathologically unconscious instances, the hands of tourists mistaking *Ursus americanus* for *Ursus Theodorus*. The intelligence and ingenuity exhibited by Yosemite bears in extracting sustenance from the aforementioned food containers are amazing and the stuff of legends. Naturally, bear/human conflicts and confrontations became daily and sometimes destructive occurrences. As always, in the long run, bear lost.

By the early 1970s the Park Service reported it was responding to "rogue" (those suspected of being repeat food thief offenders) bears by trapping, drugging and "relocating." This seemed both humane and practical. Then, in the early 1970s, climber Chris Vandiver was searching out new climbing areas below the Crane Flat road when he stumbled onto the graveyard of rogue bears. He found the rotting carcasses of dozens of bears the Park Service had killed before furtively dumping their bodies off a cliff from the Crane Flat Road. Vandiver told Galen Rowell about it and Galen photographed and wrote it up, embarrassing the Park Service but forcing them to seek other solutions to the "bear problem." While the Park Service's assertion that it was "relocating" the bears was, from one pint of view, correct, the impression it fostered was misleading, dishonest and disgusting, while at the same time giving its flack men the illusion of deniability.

We would understand immediately and turn away with a certain horror from all those activities that violate the integrity of the planet.

To say nothing of the integrity of the people who relocated the bears as well as the mouthpieces who covered for them. Having the ability to find deniability in the undeniable bamboozling of the citizenry, to say nothing of hiding the graveyards of bears and other creatures, including honorable soldiers in caskets, seems to be a requisite for long-term government employment.

To their credit, the Park Service has since installed hundreds of steel bear proof storage containers and garbage deposits all over Yosemite Valley, causing bears to work harder for their supper but giving both bears and people a better chance to live together. So far as we can tell, the Park Service is no longer relocating large numbers of bears, rogue or otherwise, at least not in Yosemite. But a few years ago Yosemite big wall climbers began stashing supplies overnight at the base of multi-day climbs to save time on the first day of climbing. It didn't take bear long to sniff out the new food location and to begin foraging along the base of Yosemite's walls for the unwatched backpack or haul bag. Though climbers and campers have for the most part learned, pickings are relatively if randomly good, as evidenced by the bears that walk through camp in the night and scavenge along the base of the walls favored by climbers. During our time there, Jeannie and Helen did the south face of Washington's column. They took a haul bag with climbing and sleeping gear but devoid of food up the fourth class ledges to the base of the climb, returning the next afternoon to spend the night before starting the climb early the following morning. They found a bear had scrambled up the fourth class ledges, ripped open their haul bag and devoured a tube of sun block cream, scattering their gear and ripping a few things in the process. They also found dozens of abandoned plastic water bottles and abundant garbage left by climbers. When they returned to Dinner Ledge after their climb, they cleaned up as many discarded plastic containers as they could carry. What they could not bring with them is the unyielding stench of urine that pervades Dinner Ledge and other ledges pissed upon by generations of Yosemite climbers. While most (but certainly not all) of my climbing friends have always practiced the ethic of hauling out our garbage and even the garbage of others when possible, more than 30 years ago I too pissed upon Dinner Ledge and other ledges of Yosemite. Everybody did. Everybody still does. What else is a climber to do? Many climbers could do a better job of picking up after themselves than they do, but the sheer numbers of climbers have turned Yosemite into what one waggish friend described (accurately, in my mind) as "the world's largest urban outdoor climbing gym." It is a fact that man is turning more and more of the planet into an urban landscape, and a good argument can be made that the values of urbanity itself violate the integrity of the planet.

One day I hiked up to Half Dome via Vernal and Nevada Falls and Little Yosemite Valley, a six and a half hour round trip workout and somewhat of a sentimental journey for me. It was an astonishing experience as hundreds of people clogged the trail as far as Vernal Fall, dozens as far as Nevada Fall. The last time I'd hiked that trail I encountered perhaps twenty people all day. Not until Little Yosemite was the hike anything other than a passage through an urban landscape. The Mist Trail below the falls was reminiscent of walking up one of San Francisco's hills on a drizzly day, except the trail was more crowded than the streets of that fair city. Indeed, the entire trail is paved to the falls, as it must be to handle such traffic. There were several groups of teen-age students accompanied by teachers. One hugely overweight young man was struggling mightily if unhappily up the stone steps. His friends were cheering him on to persevere and it was not clear that he would be able to do so. The support of the fat boy's friends was commendable and encouraging, but it occurred to me that one manifestation of the pathology to which Thomas Berry refers is the overabundance of young people in our society for whom walking uphill for a couple of miles on a fine spring California day is agony instead of pleasure, a major accomplishment instead of a ritual of healthy living. It is a safe bet that that young man in the bloom of youth did not notice a like bloom on the landscape around him.

I was happy to reach Little Yosemite simply because it was the first remotely non-urban experience I'd had since driving into Yosemite Valley more than a week earlier. The previous sentence was written in full awareness that the automobile itself is an integral part of modern man's urban value system. Like everyone reading this, I am a modern man and part of the problem, and, if there is a solution short of the not out of the question extinction of mankind, part of the solution. There were only a few hikers in Little Yosemite, but I was surprised to see a Park Service log cabin that had appeared since I had last been there. I wandered along at my own pace and took in the great south face of Half Dome and reminisced about my friends Galen Rowell and Warren Harding, both now dead, and of their fine first ascent of the south face and of their epic rescue off that face on their first storm bound attempt. The air was hazy, but it was wonderful to feel something of the spiritual glow that infused John Muir's Yosemite and which I missed with pangs of homesickness. I stopped to eat lunch on a boulder before heading up the trail to the east shoulder below the cable to the summit. I passed only one other hiker coming down, but when I got beneath the cable I was treated to a surprising sight: some 15 or 20 people were strung out along the cable, both ascending and descending. The cable was not yet up and was lying against the rock, so hikers were forced to bend over to hold on as they went up, or, with more difficulty, came down. As is the case in all endeavors, some were having an easier time than others. One gentleman seemed to have panicked half way up the cable and was spread out on the rock with a two hand death grip on the cable and both feet off the rock. People both ascending and descending were stopped, trying to help the hapless hiker. He didn't move for some 10 minutes before being coaxed/ aided to retreat back down the cable. I watched the Half Dome cable summit scene for awhile before deciding that it was too crowded for my mood that day. I had been there before and perhaps would again, but I turned around and went back down to the valley.

We climbed the superb rock of Yosemite a few more days. Three of our more hard core friends from Jackson Hole drove straight through from Wyoming, slept for seven hours, and in the next three days climbed three different routes on El Capitan and then drove non-stop back to Jackson. We were impressed. On our last day we climbed the moderate, classic Nutcracker Suite, a route I'd done many times. We had a hard time finding a place to park because a television commercial was being filmed and vans, equipment trucks, cameramen, actors, actresses, grips, directors and the entire scene that sells consumerism to America had taken over the area. We unloaded our climbing gear and walked through a very urban atmosphere to Manure Pile Buttress. We had a fine time on Nutcracker. The polishing of the route was noticeable, not surprising as we were one of five parties on the route at the same time, two Italians in front of us, two Germans behind, all good fellows and fine conversationalists on the belays, which were, to say the least, crowded.

After the climb we left Yosemite. It was late afternoon. During the week we were in Yosemite Tioga Pass was opened and we took that route east. As I guided my gas guzzling van up the Crane Flat road towards Tioga I reflected on Yosemite Valley today. The National Park Service in Yosemite and elsewhere has a mandate to "provide for the enjoyment of the visitor" and, at the same time, "leave the park unimpaired for future generations." Enjoyment is a personal, subjective matter, and one man's enjoyment is another man's agony. I question whether the Park Service can or even should be asked to provide for the enjoyment of visitors, especially if, as is the case, in the process the park becomes impaired. And there is no question that Yosemite Valley, like the other National Parks, is impaired. The two metaphors that stick in my mind about Yosemite today are the television commercial crew and equipment and the opaque air that even Ansel Adams could not have seen through to clarity. The crowds are not a metaphor but, rather, the state of planet earth and both cause and effect of the disturbance at a basic level of consciousness to which Berry refers. It is not the Park Service's fault that Yosemite has become a polluted, crowded, urban traffic jam, or that snowmobiles inundate Yellowstone, or that the air in the Smoky Mountains is among the worst in America. It is the fault of man's collective trivializing attitude toward the earth. Climbers are as much to blame for Yosemite's degradation as the Winnebago crowd, the tour bus circuit, the Park Service itself, the concessionaires, the oil/automobile industries and the spineless members of the U.S. Congress for whom the environment and National Parks are only another business opportunity for their campaign contributors. I do not know what it will take to heal Yosemite, but each of us, climber and non-climber alike can do something—learn to leave no trace, carry out trash and feces, don't join the crowd, turn away in horror from that which violates integrity, monitor the trivializing attitude. Get involved. Write a letter. Phone a Congressman. Get pissed. Such small intentions may not take care of the problem, which is humungous, but they will benefit the practitioner, who is sacred. Personally, I favor more drastic measures. Yosemite will not be healed until all the roads into the valley are closed, all vehicles banned, all houses and lodges and restaurants and permanent tents removed. Let people who want to see the Yosemite walk into the valley, climbers included. To those who level the charge of elitism to such ideas, I reply that the idea that the wonders of the world are worth some effort to see and to keep unimpaired, and the notion that they are available to everyone with the skill and strength to sit in a seat, step on a gas pedal, steer an automobile and pay for a tank of gas is one that trivializes the planet and makes of it an economic resource and place of recreation, empty of spiritual glow.

Let them walk.

Let us all walk.

Let Yosemite have a rest. Give the earth a rest. But even banning automobiles in Yosemite is a stop-gap measure, one that should be put in place. It is man's trivializing attitude toward the very nature which sustains him that needs changing. Banning cars in Yosemite may give him some time to make those changes and learn to turn away with a certain horror from all those activities that violate the integrity of the planet.

Such thoughts bubbled away in my brain even as I guided the van along the Tioga road. I talked to Jeannie about the week in Yosemite and of what we had experienced and about the crowds. We had some fine climbing and a good time in one of our favorite spots. We were leaving with both satisfying and unsettling memories and impressions. We talked about how the earth and all its creatures are suffering from man's blind cleverness. We enjoyed the talk and the drive and each other's company and the memories we shared.

A few miles before reaching Tuolumne Meadows a medium-size very black bear burst out of the trees on the right and ran across the road in front of us. This bear was beautiful and healthy and fast and on a mission to somewhere. It was a thrilling sight, but around his neck was a bright blue radio collar, and no bear can ever go home again with a collar around its neck.

PART TWO

Climbers

CHAPTER TEN

Barry Corbet
1936 – 2004

A few days after Barry Corbet's not unexpected death from bladder cancer in December 2004 a letter arrived to many of his friends. It was from Barry telling them that he treasured their friendships, a nice touch to the end of a rich and significant life well lived. Barry's words from that letter are the best illustration of the depth and richness of that life and the quality of his person: "I'm a little saddened to be leaving a little earlier than expected, but feel no sense of tragedy. I've lived a lot longer than I ever could have or would have predicted thirty-six years ago after the helicopter crash. I have no fears for my children, who are all embarked on their own roads and doing it with astounding style and grace. I've had love overflowing, impassioned careers, a life of adventure and everything I've ever wanted. Nothing missed and no regrets.

"So, dear friends, enjoy the memories, keep them alive, then let them fade when it's time. Live on in peace, health and happiness. Look for meaning where you can and cherish mystery where you can't."

That was Barry Corbet who built a life and his first careers out of adventure in the mountains until a 1968 helicopter crash left him paralyzed from the waist down. Born and raised in Vancouver, B.C., he moved to the U.S. to attend Dartmouth College, an institution from which he dropped out several times in order to pursue impassioned careers and a life of climbing and skiing adventure. Eventually Barry moved west and settled in Jackson Hole, Wyoming.

He guided for Exum Mountain Guides for 10 years and ran a climbing store, the Outhaus, with partners Jake Breitenbach and Dick Pitman. He taught skiing in Jackson Hole and with his wife, Mary (Muffy), ran the Alpenhorn Lodge. As a climber Barry had many first ascents to his credit all over the world, including the South Ridge of Baxter's Pinnacle, one of the most popular routes in the Tetons, the Southwest Rib of Denali and Mt. Tyree in the Antarctic. It is authoritatively rumored that he was part of the secret CIA-sponsored expedition to Nanda Devi in the Himalaya to plant a surveillance device on the summit for monitoring China's nuclear tests in the Takla Makan desert. He did the first ski traverse from the Bugaboos to Rogers Pass in Canada, a classic ski tour now known as "The Grand Traverse." The skier's test piece Corbet's Couloir in Jackson Hole is named for Barry.

In 1963 Barry was a member of the American expedition to Mt. Everest which put the first Americans on the summit. He had an opportunity to have a summit spot, but he gave it up to a teammate, assuming he would have another opportunity in the future. That never happened.

He was a filmmaker, writer, editor, and, for many years, a fearless paraplegic kayaker. After his accident (while making a film) he co-produced more than 100 films. He wrote many articles and publications, including his classic book "Options: Spinal Cord Injury and the Future" which insisted that disability did not preclude a good and full life. In "Options" he wrote, "There's too much fun here. I can't hold it all in. Later on, I thought the same thing skiing waist-deep powder snow in Jackson Hole, climbing mountains in Antarctica, floating in the arms of peyote back when it was still legal and kayaking after my accident. When your cup of rewards runneth over, it's a good time. My cup still runs over about as often as anyone else's. So will yours."

That was my friend, Barry Corbet.

Warren Harding.   *painting Sean McCabe*

CHAPTER ELEVEN

Batso Unbound
1924 – 2002

"DICK," WARREN HARDING SAID TO ME, "you look like a fucking insurance salesman."

"Warren," I replied, "you look like an old, broken-down climber."

It had been nearly ten years since I'd seen him, and the great climbing legend was now nearly seventy years old and alcoholic. But despite the distended belly and the shrinking frame, he was easily recognizable. No one looked like Warren Harding: the furrowed face, the deep set eyes, the slow movements of his body and the shaggy gray hair reflected more difficult miles and adventures than you could find in a library of hard-core adventure books. He looked like an old man who had well used and abused his years, not like one who had been used and abused by them.

I was the one who'd become hard to recognize. In the years since we'd last tipped wine glasses together, I'd shorn a thirteen-year growth of beard and retired from the drinking/drugging life and even had a full-time job half the year, though that would last only another half year.

I'd been living in Aspen and climbing around Moab, when I heard rumors that Warren had moved to town from California. Then he came looking for me and left a phone number at the climbing store and a friend of a friend got the number to me. The next morning I called and soon found myself at the kitchen table of an unremarkable suburban Moab house in the company of Warren and his companion

Alice Fromp. The decade's changes duly noted, we picked up where we'd left off, Alice and Warren sipping watered-down white wine, me sipping watered-down water. Alice, twice Warren's size on the horizontal plane, doted on him in a charming manner, keeping his glass full, laughing at all his jokes, treating me as an old friend though we had only met that morning. We talked about mutual friends, climbing (of course), living in the desert, writing, writers, the vagaries of life, the follies of men and the pretentious pomposities of a select few of the self-important ones.

As I had remembered, Warren's insight, wit and fierce independence of thought were more fun and enlightening than the more rigid and predictable views of some of his fundamentalist critics. He reiterated that morning a viewpoint I had heard before and which he expanded in his wonderful, satirical book *Downward Bound: A Mad Guide to Rock Climbing* and in the few issues of his unique periodical *Descent*: "Climbing is such a stupid fucking activity, what is wrong with people who take it (and themselves) so fucking seriously that they want to institutionalize it. We climb to be free, not to moralize about something as stupid as climbing a rock. People are hopeless, so we might as well have some fun."

True, a conversation with Warren, especially when the wine flowed, which was often, could be as unorthodox and unpredictable as the slide show/lecture on Yosemite big wall climbing he once gave at The Passage Bar and Restaurant in Truckee. He had put the slides together hurriedly and had not rehearsed his talk. It was a raucous full house that gathered in the Passage that early 1980s night and by the time Warren was ready to perform both audience and lecturer were primed, so to speak. The lights dimmed, the audience quieted, the first slide appeared on the screen, appropriately enough a beautiful shot of El Capitan, the Nose in profile. But the vertical slide had been inserted in the carousel horizontally and El Cap was lying on its side. "Whoops," said Warren, "you'll have to tilt your head to the side and you can see just as well." Both Warren and the entire audience laughed, tilted their heads to the side while he led them through the first ascent of El Cap and more, much of it out of sequence. And, the thing was, in the end, after sufficient laughter, hooting, sidetracks and non sequiturs, the audience had learned as much about Yosemite big-wall climbing and climbers, the motivations that impelled them and the values they truly lived by as they would have gleaned from more traditional and stern accounts of the same climbs. But Harding's audiences had a lot more fun and had to do a lot more thinking, though their necks and heads might be a bit stiff in the morning.

That's something of how a conversation at a kitchen table over watered down wine and watered down water could be with Warren Harding, and for the first couple of hours I thoroughly enjoyed it. He was particularly funny that morning talking about a mutual (old) climbing friend who had apparently lived in the house with him and Alice for a time, but the old friend drank too much for Warren's tastes. "Can you believe it," he said, "—got so drunk he passed out on the couch and wouldn't go to bed? Can you believe that? We had to kick him out." And he laughed the laugh of the satirist making fun of himself, but not only himself. But then the wine drowned the water and Warren began to repeat himself and lose track and not make even farcical sense any longer, and, you know, there's nothing worse for an ex-drinker than trying to talk with an old drinking buddy who has rounded the corner (usually around the third or fourth glass of wine) to irrelevant repetition and the meandering sidetrack of indefinite certainty, indecipherable allusions and elliptical elocution, especially when the ex-drinker is aware of the vast karmic debt of indecipherable allusions and elliptical elocution he does not remember but somehow knows he has incurred. Fortunately, Warren was generous of heart. I liked him very much and wanted to spend more time with the Warren of the first part of the day.

"Say," I interrupted him in mid-sentence, "why don't we go climbing?"

He stopped speaking and regarded me with a wild-ass look. "No, no, I couldn't do that. I don't climb any more," he said, his eyes drifting away from mine.

"Sure you could," I insisted with a smile. "I know a spot right on the road where we can set up a top rope and the climbs are not hard and we'll have a great time. We can do a few laps and have a workout. You'll love it."

"No no no, I'm doing good to climb out of bed in the morning," he said, but I could see his interest was aroused. His slouch over the table straightened ever so perceptibly.

Alice saw it too. She knew her man and smiled to see his posture change. "Warren, you should go climbing with Dick," she said. "That's a great idea. Yes, Warren, go climbing."

"Wellll-l-l-l-l-llllll … "

An hour later we were at the School Room of Wall Street along the Colorado River, after a full twenty-foot approach from my car. I set up top ropes on two routes in the 5.7–5.8 range. Warren had resurrected from his basement a ratty old harness and a tired-looking pair of climbing shoes and he tied in and leapt upon the lovely sandstone of Utah with an impressive if initially shaky fervor. He struggled on the first lap, his feet slipped off even big holds, his hands didn't grip, his fingers slipped off and he hung on the rope every two or three moves. When he got down he wanted a break and a drink of water, which he got. He belayed me and then he took another lap on the same route. This time he began to move with the practiced if rusty grace of a battered seventy-year-old body that has spent its life climbing rock. As the memory of physical movement returned and his mind sobered, Warren's famous satanic visage became radiant. The soul of the soul of the golden age of Yosemite big-wall climbing had reappeared. All the merriment of having broken free of the institutions of old age, alcoholism, society's stupidity and lack of exercise showed in a smile that can only come from the heart.

"That was really fun," he said. After a rest and some water, we climbed some more. The first time he tried the 5.8 Warren fell off and hung a few times. The last time he climbed the entire route without a slip, a hesitation or any observable undue strain. As we packed up our gear he told me that it had been an "inspiring" afternoon and that he was going to start hiking and get back in shape. I believed him and told him of some of the hikes I knew around Moab. He said that if he started hiking some, he should be able to do some easy climbing around the area. I told him there were undoubtedly some local climbers who would be happy to show him around. All he had to do was go to the gear shop and let it be known that he wanted to climb. If he got himself in shape, I told him, I'd love to drive over from Aspen and climb the 5.6 route on South Six Shooter Peak in Indian Creek with him. He said he was going to do just that, but in the way of old friends whose lives are on different trajectories, I never saw Warren again. It never became clear to me why they had forsaken their beloved California for Moab, Utah, but in any case their sojourn in the desert didn't last long. Perhaps a new start in life? We spoke by phone a few times over those years but I don't know whether he hiked himself back into shape or ever climbed again. I hope he did. After Warren died on February 27, 2002 in Anderson, California, Alice told the San Francisco Chronicle, "We went on a six-city tour in Canada in 1988, and I was just amazed at all the people who turned out to see his slide shows. They just loved him."

And they did.

When I drove Warren back to his house in Moab, he was calm, even contemplative (he was also probably really fatigued). He didn't talk much on the drive home and when I asked if he wanted to stop somewhere for a drink he said "no," and I had the thought that he was a man who had been dragged out of retirement for an afternoon to do the work that he was meant to do, the work that defined his life and was in many ways the best part of that life, the work that gave him the deepest satisfaction and best insight into himself. Alice was happy to see him and Warren to see her and they hugged each other with tender affection not usually associated with the hard-man/hedonist/satirist/cynic Warren Harding.

My last view and memory of Warren Harding is that of a complex man who had beaten back his demons for an afternoon by nothing more complicated than battering them against a slab of sandstone above the Colorado River by Potash Road. He was calm, content and happy. He stood a bit straighter than he had that morning and to my mind his frame was solid, his belly flatter and his smile devilishly radiant.

Galen & Barbara Rowell with the Dalai Lama.

photo courtesy Mountain Light

CHAPTER TWELVE

Galen (1940 – 2002)
& Barbara (1948 – 2002)

IN 1969 I WAS WALKING ALONG THE BASE OF EL CAPITAN in the lovely Yosemite with a couple of climbing buddies when we ran into Galen Rowell. I was new to climbing and not up on my Yosemite climbing history and had never heard Galen's name, but we were introduced and I was immediately struck by the fierce intensity of his person. His handshake was firm, his smile sincere, and there was a gleeful, wild passion in his eyes that I liked and trusted from the very beginning. We climbed together part of that day and began a friendship that endured and immeasurably enriched and informed my life.

Galen Rowell immeasurably enriched and informed the lives of many people. I believe Galen's work has enriched and made more secure the lives of all the creatures which inhabit the earth. I say this because that work has raised man's awareness of the beauty, the inherent dignity, the fragility and the spiritual dimension of the wild places, the wild creatures, and the wild people of the world. As we all know, too many of the wild places are being polluted and destroyed, too many of the wild creatures are either domesticated or on the verge of extinction, and far too many of the wild people are becoming corporate executives. Only human awareness can save the wild, and we need the wild.

We need the wild in order to survive. Nature needs the wild in order to be nature. We need the wild as individuals, as a people (Americans in our case), as members of the biological community of the planet (Homo sapiens). Galen's images, writings, activism and the path of his life are reminders to us of that need. There are others better qualified to comment on Galen's contributions and accomplishments in the climbing world, and others still who know far more about the skill and beauty and ultimate value of his photography and writing. But as his friend I can say that the essence and source of his success, accomplishment and vision was in that wild passion he brought to whatever he was doing. I have known very few people with the kind of energy and ability to focus in the moment as Galen Rowell. Whether he was climbing, taking photographs, giving a talk, discussing the ideas of Konrad Lorenz, the observations of John McPhee, the music of Villa Lobos, or taking one of his power runs in the Berkeley Hills, life was always an adventure for him. And, of course, anyone who was ever in an automobile with Galen at the wheel knows that driving with him was always a memorable adventure for his passengers.

It has been one of the great privileges of my life to have shared some of that adventure with Galen—in his beloved Sierra, in the Rockies, in China and Tibet, and, of course, in Berkeley and Yosemite.

In the mid 1970s I was working as a ski coach in Squaw Valley. A woman named Barbara Cushman was involved in a small clothing company called SPACE COWBOY, and she wanted to make ski parkas for our coaches. I met her and her handshake was firm, her smile sincere (and beautiful), and there was a no bullshit honesty in her eyes that I liked and trusted immediately. She said she would make (and sell) us the best parkas we had ever seen. True to her word, as always, she did. All the coaches cherished and stayed warm in our SPACE COWBOY parkas. A couple of years later she had left behind her SPACE COWBOY phase of life and was working for the North Face when we met again and she became a good friend. Barbara was a rare and charming combination of toughness and vulnerability, personal ambition and concern for the world, playfulness and seriousness. Like Galen, she had a wild and deep source of energy and a great ability to focus on the task at hand. As a businesswoman she could drive a hard bargain, but she always believed in what she was doing and she always delivered the best. Barbara strove for excellence with integrity in everything. Those two words—excellence and integrity—come easily to mind when thinking of Barbara Cushman Rowell. She was a loyal and wonderful friend to me, and we had a lot of good times and many laughs together.

When Galen and Barbara met in 1981 at the North Face, it was love at first sight. They immediately embarked on a phenomenal partnership. Like every relationship, theirs was not without difficult times, but I consider Barbara and Galen to be one of the true great love stories of our circle of friends. In so many ways they were a perfect match. The most obvious example is that while Galen provided the images that made Mountain Light what it is, it was Barbara who made the business of Mountain Light what it is. They supported, encouraged, prodded and pushed each other in the life long project of continuing to grow, continuing to learn, and continuing to expand their personal horizons and capabilities.

Sometime in the late 1980s I noticed that I seldom thought of Galen alone or of Barbara alone. I thought of them as Barbara and Galen, Galen and Barbara, a unit, an entity larger and more significant than the sum of the two of them. And to the end, that entity of those two beautiful people continued to grow and to explore and experience life with wild passion and no-bullshit honesty.

We should all do as well.

And there is this: a few years ago the Yosemite Institute hosted an event in Galen's honor. I was asked to say a few words. Though I had planned on saying something else, on the spur of the moment I took that opportunity to publicly thank Galen and Barbara for being my friends for many years, for their support and encouragement in some very bad times, and for sharing in the good ones. I told them I deeply valued their presence on this earth, and I thanked them for enriching and informing my life. I am so very glad and grateful that I did that when I had the chance, for there will never be another.

It seems to me that the most meaningful, living tribute each of us could offer to Galen and Barbara is to make the extra effort to keep in touch with those who have mattered in our lives and to make sure they know they matter. Keep in touch with old friends. Keep in touch with new friends. Keep in touch with adventure. Keep in touch with passion. Keep in touch with the wild. Keep in touch. Keep in touch. Keep in touch.

And say "thank you" for family, and "thank you" for friendship while you can.

Thank you.

CHAPTER THIRTEEN

Paul Petzoldt
1908 – 1999

THE FIRST TIME PAUL PETZOLDT took the responsibility of guiding someone in the Sawtooth Mountains of central Idaho was in 1920. He led a friend and his dog, Ranger, on a tour of the Sawtooth and later wrote of the experience, "Perhaps it was then I realized the mountains and wilderness were indispensable to me," In 1920 Paul Petzoldt was 12 years old.

From that time until his death in 1999 at the age of 91 Petzoldt was a true pioneer of American mountaineering, wilderness education, conservation and the culture of mountain living. Born in Creston, Iowa in 1908, he was raised on a farm by the Snake River in southern Idaho. His impressive climbing resume includes climbing Wyoming's Grand Teton at the age of 16 in cowboy boots, a near disastrous adventure that convinced him that he needed to learn a great deal more if he was to continue as a mountaineer. He realized that better training, preparation and techniques were essential to survival in the mountains and he became a pioneer in these areas in his own climbing and, ultimately, in teaching others. That he learned well is shown in the fact that he climbed the Grand Teton in 1984, on the 60th anniversary of his first ascent. He tried again on the 70th anniversary in 1994 when he was 86 and suffering from glaucoma, reaching 11,000 feet before deciding that was enough for a blind octogenarian. In between were hundreds of ascents of the Grand Teton and many other mountains.

In the 1930s Petzoldt was on the first American expedition to K2 in the Himalaya and set a record for living above 20,000 feet for the longest time. On this same expedition he was the first to reach 8,000 meters on the Abruzzi Spur of K2. In 1936 he and his brother Curly and Fred Brown made the first winter ascent of the Grand Teton. He also did a one-day double traverse of the Matterhorn on the Swiss/Italian border. The Petzoldt Couloir on Idaho's Mt. Heyburn which rises above Redfish Lake is named after him and he climbed it in 1947, but it is not clear that his was the first ascent.

He was a professional guide as a teenager and in 1929 he began climbing with Glenn Exum in the Teton Mountains and they formed the Petzoldt-Exum Guide Service which still exists as Exum Mountain Guides. During World War II Petzoldt was an instructor with the Army's Tenth Mountain Ski Division ski troops at Camp Hale, Colorado. Bigger than life in both physical size and prowess, gregarious and a natural (and practiced) storyteller, Petzoldt was a man who always forged his own path and thereby helped others do the same.

Contact with other climbers and climbing guides convinced Petzoldt that, while many of them were excellent climbers, they knew little about conservation practices, safety in the mountains, expedition planning or teaching wilderness skills to others, He once wrote, "Almost from the beginning of my guiding career, I had the desire not only to guide my clients but to teach them as well." He helped establish the first American Outward Bound program in Colorado, and in 1965 he established in Lander, Wyoming The National Outdoor Leadership School (NOLS), the first American school specifically designed to train wilderness educators. NOLS mission statement declares it was "... to train leaders capable of conducting all-round wilderness programs in a safe and rewarding manner."

His timing was perfect. The 60s in America was a time of turmoil, cultural reevaluation and mass protests, and many young people were marginalized and even shunned by mainstream America. He was the right man in the right place at the right time because, as John Gans, Executive Director of NOLS said, "He had a great belief in young people.... There was Petzoldt, in his 50s, taking kids with long hair into the mountains. He believed in their potential as leaders; he believed that if given a chance, they'd do great things. He built an organization on it, and he built his life on it ... His contributions to the youth of America, to wilderness and to the development of leaders is unparalleled."

Petzoldt was married four times but had no children. He considered his students as his children. Any man who has been married four times obviously has an appreciation for women, and among Petzoldt's legacies is that of being the first to put women in positions of leadership in wilderness education. Diane Shoutis, NOLS graduate and Alumni Relations Coordinator, said "Paul empowered us with confidence in ourselves to make decisions. He was a man among men, leading the way and encouraging women to try new things."

Neil Short, a Casper, Wyoming attorney and NOLS graduate, said, "NOLS alumni are leaders in many different (areas)—in industry and politics. The impact on my life is hard to measure. There's something that's longer lasting than mountaineering skills and wilderness expeditioning skills. Perhaps the greatest talk that Paul would give was not about technique or about technical aspects of mountaineering, or about fly fishing or wilderness travel. The greatest talk he would give was about expedition behavior—how to get along with one another. It was actually a short course on how to view life."

Jeff Niwa and Fred Beckey.   *photo Reid Dowdle*

CHAPTER FOURTEEN

Encounters with Fred
(dirtbag lessons)

THE TERM "DIRTBAG" HAS CONNOTATIONS both pejorative and
flattering, like the word "bad" or "BAD," and whether the label is praise
or put down is not always clear. On occasion it can be both at the
same time, but when the dirtbag stamp has been applied, just as when
a climber refers to a route as "interesting," it generally indicates that
calling up more than the usual powers of attention is a good idea. There
is always more to (and in) the dirtbag than meets the cursory glance.

In some circles of the climbing world the dirtbag lifestyle is both
honorable and much admired. Its protocols are more concerned with
improvising practical solutions to life's kaleidoscopic challenges than
with the delineated canons of conventional consumer respectability.
As climbing in America gained status, numbers and mainstream
respectability in the past couple of decades, the dirtbag became rarer.
It is, after all, a demanding life style to maintain. For most dirtbag
climbers it is a passing phase of life, later looked back upon through
good old days filters with affection, nostalgia and sometimes longing.
Only a few rare birds persevere. One retired dirtbag American climber
who no longer climbs and who is a multimillionaire businessman,
was recently described in an article as "still a dirtbag." Apparently, this
absurd assertion was made because he sleeps on the ground from time to
time while indulging in outdoor recreation activities in places as diverse
as Patagonia, Hawaii and Iceland and often dresses in casual sport
clothes more than two years old. The millionaire dirtbag is a fantasy

found only in the pages of Men's Journal, Esquire, Vogue, Outside and the like. A genuine, living dirtbag lifestyle has authentic consequences for blinking that simply do not exist for someone with a secure bank account and personal/social/material interests and responsibilities beyond the life style and its underlying goal. In climbing, that goal is to climb. Committed, life-time dirtbag climbers are extraordinary and few and usually eccentric as hell, though it is inconceivable that the species would ever become extinct.

Whatever the status of the order the undisputed King of American dirtbag climbers is Fred Beckey. So far as I know Beckey has more first ascents in more mountain ranges than any other American climber. The quality and scope of his career, as evidenced by his routes and the purity of intention, spirit and integrity of his climbing, have no equal. His first major first ascent was in 1938. He is the original, the standard and the best, and he has managed to pull it off with the style and grace of a king. In pure climbing terms, the lifestyle, like Beckey himself, works. John Middendorf wrote of a first ascent of an Alaskan peak he did with the 74 year old Beckey in 1995:

> I was quite impressed with Fred: still as sharp as a tack when it comes to logistics of an expedition, and incredibly fit. The first day we hiked over 8 miles on up and down terrain with pretty heavy packs (with only a little complaining). Of course, all his gear is archaic: frame packs, leather boots, and neoprene strap crampons.... Fred's endurance of carrying heavy loads in his ancient frame pack amazed me....We climbed Peak 8500 on June 28th in whiteout, windless conditions. Just prior to roping up on the upper Cathedral glacier, Fred fell into a deep crevasse to his neck, and was heroically rescued by Calvin, who leaped over the crevasse in a flash and pulled Fred out. The crux of the route was a loose rock step, which Fred led (5.5X). It was nice to climb with Fred, with all his experiences in the mountains, and with whom every logistical aspect of climbing and living in the mountains was at all times thought out in detail. From the rock step a beautiful snow ridge led to the summit. The three of us had been alternating leads during the climb, and although Fred had been leading on the section

*just below the top, he stopped 20 feet short of the summit and allowed
me to pass, in honor of it being my first Alaskan summit, whereupon
I named the peak Mt. Beckey."*

At this writing, Beckey is almost 80 and still climbing. Just three years
ago he climbed Mt. Moran in the Teton Range, an arduous task at any
age.

In 1969 I was sitting in Yosemite's Camp 4, dirtbag heaven for
American climbers of the time, when a tall, lovely, coiffed, groomed,
athletic, well-dressed in clean clothes, blonde woman with blue eyes
and a face to make angels weep with joy walked by my camp site. She
was stunningly beautiful. While many beautiful women have walked
through and even stayed in Camp 4, this one possessed an elegance and
careful appearance not usually seen among the au natural women who
traditionally resided in and passed through the dusty sites of that free-
form, free-spirited community. I was momentarily mesmerized by the
sight of this lovely woman moving over the earth before noticing she
was not alone. Another woman and two men accompanied her. Damn.
And then I came to my senses and realized that one of the men was my
old friend the ski photographer Dick Barrymore, among the last people
I would expect to see in Camp 4. I hailed him and met his companions
and discovered what he was doing in Yosemite. The stunning blonde was
Betsy Glenn who soon would marry Dick and become Betsy Barrymore.
The other woman was the other man's weekend date and the other man
was Fred Beckey. He, too, had a face to make angels weep, though not
exactly with joy. His countenance was lined and creased and weathered
by a lifetime of climbing routes of unimaginable difficulty, routes in the
mountains, routes within. It is a face reflecting the unending struggle of
what it is to be a human being.

At the time I had been climbing for only a year, but even I had
heard Fred Beckey stories. Famous climber. Hard man. King of the
dirtbags. A man constantly on the move. He called Seattle home but was
as likely to be found exploring the sandstone towers of the southwest
deserts, the glaciers of Alaska, the fine granite of the Sawtooth, or in

an automobile en route between them as bushwhacking through the northwest's temperate rainforest jungles. I had heard how he shopped at the Seattle Goodwill and Salvation Army stores to buy a few dozen second hand neckties and a heavy wool overcoat for a couple of dollars before climbing expeditions. He bivouacked in the overcoat, leaving it in the woods or on the crags at his last camp and he used the neckties to tie off pitons on tricky aid pitches. The overcoats would keep a camper warm in a wet storm, the neckties would hold a small fall, and both were cheap and expendable solutions to a couple of the problems of climbing on a meager budget. I've often wondered about the thoughts of northwest backpackers who found a moldy old overcoat and some silk neckties in the dirt at the base of some granite wall 20 miles from the nearest road. I also knew Beckey was famous for picking up climbing partners wherever/however/whomever he could. But Dick Barrymore, the ski photographer?

It turned out that Barrymore was a major source of income for Beckey in those years. Among the ways Fred made enough money to support his lifestyle was organizing Dick's ski films and lectures in the Northwest. Dick attracted large crowds of skiers to his shows, and his films helped finance unknowable numbers of Beckey's new climbing routes, making Dick a significant if unknowing patron of American climbing. Fred was taking Dick and Betsy on a little recreational climbing trip as a friend. His date for the weekend didn't climb, so Fred, Dick, Betsy and I climbed "After Six," a classic Yosemite 5.6 climb on Manure Pile Buttress, the first time I ever climbed with Beckey and the only time with Dick or Betsy. We left his date at the base of the climb but that night we all gathered to cook and eat our different dinner menus at a Camp 4 table. Fred's date was a city girl, clearly unfamiliar with the culture, lifestyle, attire and cuisine of places like Camp 4. She was a good sport about most of it, but it was never clear to me how she came to be with Fred. They didn't seem all that familiar with each other. I remember her look of incomprehension when Fred brought out two cans of Chef Boyardee spaghetti and meat balls for dinner. She was not expecting dinner from a can, was not happy about the prospect, was not familiar nor impressed with the Chef Boyardee brand of fine dining, and she said so. The sad expression on Fred's unforgettable weathered old face said it all: he had sincerely planned on impressing her and truly wished to please her. Incomprehension over his date's lack of appreciation for the dirtbag mountaineer gourmand's dinner was written on his face and easy to read. It was enough to make a man yearn for the simple and straightforward task of climbing a mountain and be free of the sticky complexities of social niceties and personal intimacies, enough to make an observer howl with laughter. I don't remember how the impasse between Fred and his date played out that night, but I never saw or thought of the Chef Boyardee brand again without thinking of the sad look on Fred's face as he contemplated his date's displeasure. Even among Camp 4 dirtbags of the late 1960s, Chef Boyardee was considered *déclassé*, that is, BAD.

During the next few years I encountered Beckey several times in various circumstances and became one of his legions of casual friends and admirers. He often popped up in conversation with other climbers (as he still does), and one of the first times I saw Galen Rowell angry was when some loose-lipped climber referred to Beckey as a "peak bagger." Galen was incensed, quickly and fiercely coming to Fred's defense, giving the thoughtless young climber a lesson in climbing history, ethics and traditions. Not long after this, Galen took one of the more memorable photos ever taken of Fred. On a climb in the southern Sierra, Galen photographed Fred shitting into a plastic bag while squatting in his aid slings on the side of a granite wall. The photo, a true classic, was made into an unrivaled back country environmental poster with the message PACK IT OUT printed on the bottom. A combination of Galen's unerring eye, the subject, the setting, but most of all the priceless face of Fred Beckey made the photo work. True dirtbags pack it out.

In "Downward Bound," Warren Harding's beautiful, irreverent, surreal and inimitably Harding mocking of the climbing world's propensity to take itself and its leading practitioners more seriously than, say, Harding ever took any of them, including himself, he makes reference to this photo: *"Mr. Beckey is the object of a complete investigation being conducted by the L.S.E.D & F. S. to determine the validity of his prodigious (claimed) climbing record-of which serious doubts have been raised. When one considers the amount of time Mr. Beckey spends driving to and from Seattle, talking on the telephone, and shitting, it seems more than likely that he has done virtually no climbing at all, despite the fact that he is reputed to be the oldest climber in the United States. Zone rating will be withheld pending completion of the inquiry."*

During the late 1970s and early 1980s I taught skiing at Squaw Valley in California. Fred used to show up on occasion and we would ski together. His skiing technique and attire were straight out of the 1950s and among the fashion conscious skiers (not all of them into high fashion) of Squaw Valley in those days Fred seemed an anomaly, a space-time traveler from another era. Fred was what he seemed in this regard, a classic and timeless explorer/adventurer/wanderer who would never find a fashionable or easy social fit in any era, in the mold of Wilfred Thesiger, Marco Polo, Alexandra David-Neel, Bill Tillman and Eric Shipton. But Fred was a good skier and I thoroughly enjoyed skiing with him, and a conversation with Fred was like being in the presence of a verbal encyclopedia without an index. You never knew what might come up next, but whatever the subject, it was discussed with intelligence and sometimes buried in an excess of details most of us miss because of impatience, laziness or a lack of care. One day while we were skiing he mentioned that he was looking for some new randonee bindings. I had a used pair of skis and randonee bindings and told him he was welcome to them. All he had to do was drop by my house at Soda Springs on Donner Summit and pick them up. He said thanks but he wasn't going that way today but he'd keep it in mind. Some two months later the phone rang at six in the morning. It was Fred from Lovelock, Nevada, having driven west all night alone from somewhere and some climb and he would be passing by Soda Springs in a few hours. Could he pick up the skis and bindings? When he dropped by I gave him the gear and we chatted for awhile before he raced off in an old automobile for some obscure destination in the Bay Area that he referred to as secretly as he guarded his future climbing projects. Beckey did not accrue all those first ascents by telling the climbing world about them in advance, and he was nearly as closed mouthed about his personal life. Perhaps he thought it was not very interesting or important to anyone else, or maybe he suspected it might be viewed like canned spaghetti and meatballs.

A few weeks later I went to the grocery store across the road from my house. The owner said a man had stopped by and since I wasn't home had left a package at the store for me. In a well used brown paper bag was a tall box containing an expensive bottle of brandy. A note from Fred thanked me for the skis and bindings. It was unexpected and I was touched and pleased by the gesture. They bindings were worth $100 or so, but they had cost me nothing and Fred knew that. I took the box home and put it on top of the refrigerator. A week later my wife at that time and I came home from a movie and decided to have a nightcap. I took Fred's gift down and opened it, anticipating a delicious hit of good brandy before bed. Instead of brandy, inside was a $3 bottle of cheap red wine. We had a great laugh and a nightcap of rot-gut red wine and a toast of true affection to Fred Beckey, King of Dirtbag Climbers.

Anyone who has ever attended a Fred Beckey slide show knows that the devil is in the details. A Beckey slide show is more like a graduate studies seminar on whatever climb or series of climbs or range of mountains he has chosen to present than light entertainment for armchair mountaineers. His presentations are not a posturing self-congratulation for a climb or climbs well done as are so many other slide shows. Fred's slide shows are meant to be and are educational, and no climber has a better grasp of his material than Beckey. If he had been a history professor his courses would have set the standard for the department. That is, except for the true intellectual and the doggedly studious students would have dreaded his courses for the rigors of their thoroughness, the standards of their integrity and the sheer volume of material presented; but no students would have a better education or more solid values regarding their subject.

I don't cross paths with Fred very often. Until last winter I hadn't seen him in nearly 20 years. Then we had dinner together at the Ketchum, Idaho restaurant Sushi On Second after he and Reid Dowdle had done a six hour ski tour north of town. He was tired and dehydrated and hungry. The first thing he asked me, after not seeing each other for 20 years, was, "Have you figured out yet why people climb?" Of course I have not, but as with other koans I am still working on it. The 79 year old then spent the evening eating, drinking copious amounts of water, telling stories about climbing and old girl friends and flirting outrageously with the young waitresses. He had to get up early the next morning to drive to Seattle. He had to be there the next night, though he didn't say exactly why. The two times I had seen him before that, in the 1980s at one of his slide shows in Sun Valley and when we both attended a talk Buckminster Fuller gave at the North Face in Berkeley just a couple of days before Fuller died, Fred was full of high speed plans, ideas and schemes for climbing in China, where I had climbed and he had not. Fred's energy and salesman's enthusiasm for the as yet undefined project was that of a man forty years younger. Five or six years ago I arrived at Idaho's City of Rocks a day after he had passed through, and his presence was still palpable. Young climbers whose parents were not yet born when Beckey made his first ascent of Mt. Waddington could talk of nothing else. "Fred Beckey was here." "Fred Beckey was here." As if King Arthur had suddenly dropped in on a distant camp of faithful knights to pay respect and encourage them to persevere in their search for the Holy Grail. He came. He climbed. He spoke to the faithful in the language of climbing, but before they could answer he roared off into the east in a ratty old car loaded with climbing and camping gear, headed for an unrevealed destination. "Dude, you should have seen him. He looked like, you know, like he'd been in the same clothes for a hundred years. And the hat, dude, the hat. You've never seen anything like it."

And then last summer, August 2002, I crossed one of Fred's old, old paths. It provided me with the most exhilarating lead I've had in several years. Six of us had congregated at Middle Baron Lake in Idaho's lovely Sawtooth Range for a few days of excellent rock climbing in a back country setting where we were unlikely to encounter other climbers. It is country that requires most of a day carrying a pack to access. Beckey country. The first morning we climbed the two fine 5.9 routes on Baron Spire in two groups of three. Jeannie Wall, Sandy Brown and I were on one rope. Reid Dowdle, Doug Colwell and Hanna North were on the other. Baron Spire is also known as Old Smoothie, and both routes up Old Smoothie end below the overhanging headwall leading to the summit. The final pitch of mixed aid and free climbing was put up, of course, by Fred Beckey on the first ascent of the spire in 1949. Fourteen bolts were placed on the first ascent, and the official rating has it A0, 5.9, but after 50 years not all the bolts are there and the state of the remnants contribute to the route's reputation of being hard, sketchy, run out, and scary. At the beginning of the day we had not determined whether we would bother with the last pitch. Many parties do not, but if we did I think we all assumed that Reid, who had done it before, would lead. Reid Dowdle is one of America's fine unsung, unknown, unpretentious hard-man climbers. His impressive climbing resume, as well as the intention, spirit and integrity of his career, are in the mold of Beckey. Indeed, Dowdle is a Beckey alumnus cum laude, and he probably has more Sawtooth experience than any other climber. Reid is a minimalist in most things, especially the description of climbing routes, and he laconically said that the last pitch of Baron Spire was "interesting."

We all paid attention and assumed that if we finished the spire he'd take that lead. More precisely, we hoped that none of us would have to.

The two 5.9 routes end at the same place a hundred feet of 4th class scrambling below the final summit overhang. Our two groups met and, since none of us except Reid had ever been there, started moving up the 4th class "just to have a look." It was one of those amorphous group decisions without much discussion that happens in the mountains when the day is long and the weather good and the only options are up or down. When we got to the base of the route I made one of those impetuous, spur-of-the-moment decisions that give life its best and sometimes worst moments. Though I was by several years the elder of this group and, partly as a consequence of that unyielding fact, in some ways its weakest climber, I saw that it was my pitch to do. "I'll do it," I said, and tied in and racked up and started to make some aid stirrups from slings and asked for a belay from Sandy. Everyone was surprised, none more than me. Reid brought me a set of well-worn aiders that looked as old as Beckey himself, and then he reclined on his back on a slab of sun-warmed granite with his camera. A wry smile highlighted a look on his face that said, "Interesting."

The route definitely goes up the wrong side of vertical. The first bolt, more than 50 years old, a quarter inch classic with a loose oval hanger, did not inspire confidence. Nevertheless, I clipped it with the quaking tenacity of impetuosity, added Reid's ratty aid slings to the mix, climbed to the top stirrup of one where I could clip the next loose bolt hanger from yesteryear, transferred the other aider to that bolt and stood in it and moved the second aider up and repeated the process. After just two primeval bolts worth of climbing, I was suddenly overcome with the cold sweat, helpless, fuck-me clarity of commitment. Now I'd done it. Now I had to do it. Why do we keep doing things like this?

Though the bolts were primitive and the hangers loose, soon I was past the overhang and onto the mere vertical. Then appeared a bolt with an oval hanger flattened against the wall, as if beaten with a hammer in frustration or fallen on with enough force to straighten out its old aluminum molecules like those of a flattened beer can. The hanger would not take a carabineer. I was able to thread a runner through the eye and tie it off and move up. A wired stopper hooked over a hangerless quarter inch bolt sufficed to get me up to the next dilapidated piece of 40s climbing technology. This one, too, was firmed to the wall by forces I did not wish to imagine. In addition, my reach was such that I was completely stretched out and lacked the reach to thread a runner through the hanger. What to do? I always carry a length of 6mm perlon cord that I use for a prusik on rappels. I untied it and it had just enough stiffness that after several attempts I was able to poke one end through the battered eye of the hanger and grab it from the other side and tie it off. I clipped in to the perlon cord, moved my aid slings up one by one and climbed to the top stirrup.

I found myself at the top of a line of 50 year old much abused bolts that did not inspire confidence placed by a man known to use neckties to tie off pitons. I was not happy, but I took consolation in remembering that Beckey has done more climbing in more places for more years than anyone without a serious accident or injury. Small solace in the moment. Not only was I in a place where the security below appeared tenuous, but there was neither foothold, handhold, nor bolt within reach above. About three feet higher than my outstretched hand was what looked like a headless nail sticking out of the wall about two inches at a slightly downward angle. After several attempts, during which time the clarity of commitment began to fog up, I managed to sort of lasso the object with a sling. Then, with conscious slow breathing, the clarity of commitment, and the gentleness and finesse reserved for A5 placements and 5.11 friction I clipped an aider into the sling and tip-toed onto the stirrup. It held. I carefully moved up one rung. It still held. I was able to tie off another sling where the broken off drill bit that looked like a nail came out of the wall at an angle that threatened to shrug off the sling that held me in place. Who knows how far the bit penetrated into the wall? Who knew its story? Beckey was no sporty bolt-gun warrior. He climbed to get up the route, not to make life more convenient for whoever wished to follow. I climbed to the top stirrups and took inventory.

No more bolts were to be seen. Beckey may have placed 14 bolts in 1949, but by 2002 some of them had shriveled up and fallen out or oxidized and blown away in the wind. It is closer to A2 than A0, and no cracks to place protection existed. Twenty feet above the angle eased off at a ramp that led to another steep headwall. "Hey, Reid," I yelled, "is there another bolt up here somewhere?"

"Yeah, I think so. Maybe....ohhh... another 30 feet. Somewhere by that ramp."

"How's the climbing to there?"

"Interesting."

Thanks Reid. I am not describing the climbing and emotions and thinking of a 25 year old 5.12 climber for whom mortality is an abstract concept, but, rather, those of a 63 year old man for whom 5.12 is an abstract concept. I haven't a clue what Beckey did there in 1949, but in 2002 I stepped out of my aid slings onto thin face holds, reached back and unclipped those slings in case I needed them further on and made a series of moves that, to paraphrase Ambrose Bierce, marvelously focused the mind. My confidence in the protection below was incomplete, and the last time I remember being that focused was 30 years earlier when I managed to not see and miss clipping two bolts in succession on the Dike Route on Tuolumne's Piwiack Dome. After that, a mistake (third in a series) would have resulted in at least a hundred-foot fall. It was the only time I've ever known my climbing partner that day, the loquacious T.M. Herbert, to be speechless. By the time I got to the ramp and a few feet of safe ground near Old Smoothie's summit I was stinking with fear and exulting in gratefulness for a small break in the action.

"Where's the bolt, Reid?"

"Oh, it's around there somewhere. You might want to take a little rest."

"I want my Mama."

And then I saw the bolt at the top of the ramp, just before it got steep again. It looked better than the others, but maybe that was just because I was so happy to find the first protection in 30 feet. Even protection is relative. I climbed up and clipped it and took some deep breaths. It was the last protection I could see before the summit, some 25 feet above, a long way off in my state of mind. But momentum encourages clarity, and soon enough I tensioned right off the bolt to a couple of tricky face moves leading to another bolt that magically appeared and easier climbing. In a few minutes I was on the top of Baron Spire. I backed up the ancient anchors and replaced some old webbing with new, and I tied myself in and relaxed. I reveled in satisfaction and relief. I thought once again of Fred. Fred Beckey was here. Fred Beckey was here. Friends, dudes, fellow countrymen, you've never seen anything like that bolt ladder. I laughed and pictured Fred's wizened old face tightened in concentration as he hand drilled that line of bolts into the unknown. I pictured him smiling at the top in 1949, a young man at the top of his game. Thanks, Fred, for a great climb.

It was a beautiful sunny day at the crest of the Sawtooth range. I could see the three Baron Lakes and in the distance Imogene Lake and a bit of the Elephant's Perch and beyond to the White Cloud Mountains. It was a view worth the climb. My friends were about to climb up and join me on the summit. I'd had an experience to remember that filled me for a time with that particular climber's insightful satisfaction and happiness that can't be found or earned in the lowlands. I was reminded once again that a person might sleep in the rain in an overcoat or in a king size bed under down comforters in a humidified room of a castle, but it is the quality of those peak (sic) experiences when not sleeping that determines whether one lives like a king or exists as a serf.

CHAPTER FIFTEEN

Another Encounter with Fred (continuing dirtbag education)

THE PHONE RANG ON A SEPTEMBER AFTERNOON. It was Joe "Jo Jo" Josephson, friend, climber, writer, editor and publisher with an interesting proposal: Fred Beckey had come to town (Bozeman) for Davy "Garbanzo" Vaughan's birthday party and reunion of Montana's "Dirty Sox Club," a guild of Montana climbers from the 1960s through the 1980s, described as "... the original Montana climbing gang." Members of the Dirty Sox Club have such piquant nicknames as "Dougald, Dog Fuck," "Mizner the Terrible," "Java Man," "Emerfuckingson," "Brio B.O.," "Dr. Z," and "Rat Hole." They are a colorful and accomplished group of climbers and if anyone has earned an honorary membership in a group named Dirty Sox it is Washington's Fred Beckey, undisputed Sovereign of American Dirtbag Climbers who has apparently done more climbing than any climber in history. One depiction of the birthday/reunion event reports that "... five bands played all day; two roasted pigs and 10 kegs of beer were consumed by ourselves and 450 of our friends." Beckey had stayed after the festivities to recuperate and was bivouacked at the Vaughan homestead just west of town. He and Joe were going climbing the next day. Would I like to join them?

Sure. Why not? I'd climbed once with Fred nearly 40 years before, and I hadn't seen him in three or four years though we'd had a few telephone and email communiqués. It was time to team up again. Besides, I seldom get to climb with someone older than me. I wondered how long it had been since Fred, who is 84, has even talked with an elder much less climbed with one; but during the long next day of a nice climb, conversations skimming in wide arcs across politics, people, climbing, skiing, Fred's next book about the 100 best climbs in North America, women (of course) and whether hitting the endless climbing road of Fred's life to Mt. Assiniboine or to Tuolumne Meadows in a day or two or three would be his best choice, I never got around to asking him that question. I would guess it's not recent and unlikely to happen again. Who would lead the hard pitches?

Early the morning of September 11, 2007 Joe picked me up. We headed to Vaughan's, no more than ten minutes behind schedule. Five minutes before reaching Davy's house Joe's cell phone rang. It was Davy calling on Beckey's behalf. Beckey was ready and wanted to know where we were at and were we coming?

"Priceless," Joe commented after hanging up. Beckey's many hundreds of ascents, including firsts of Forbidden Peak in the Cascades in 1940 and Devil's Thumb in 1946, as well as the 2nd ascent of Mt. Waddington in 1942 were not accomplished by being patient with dawdlers.

A few minutes later we pulled into Davy's driveway to be greeted by the peerless Friedrich Wolfgang Beckey. On the ground were a ratty old canvas tie string pack and a pair of walking ski poles. Fred looked and moved like an 84 year old man with a bad back, bent at the waist as if leaning into 70 years of gale force winds that will not deter him from his calling. His unkempt thinning mane of graying but far from white hair made him look more like an iconic physics professor than the world's oldest, most prolific mountaineer. Fred's craggy visage was a stark contrast to Joe's smooth, bald pate and unlined, round face. Fred greeted us with his trademark smile that could pass for and, who knows?, might be a grimace and the twinkling eyes of a fervent intelligence that misses little of what attracts its interest and collects less of what does not. I have written elsewhere that Beckey "... had a face to make angels weep, though not exactly with joy. His countenance was lined and creased and weathered by a lifetime of climbing routes of unimaginable difficulty, routes in the mountains, routes within. It is a face reflecting the unending struggle of what it is to be a human being." Fred Beckey's face is, truly, inimitable.

Vaughan couldn't climb with us, but he came out of his handsome house to chat and wish us a good day. Soon we had Fred and his gear loaded into Joe's Volvo and Joe was driving us up Gallatin Canyon on U.S. Highway 191 in the traffic of the most dangerous highway in western America to Gallatin Tower. Sure enough, conversation skimmed in wide arcs across several topics, but Fred Beckey did not become the most inexhaustible climber in history by getting sidetracked into easy conversations not central to his mission. Mt. Assiniboine was on his mind, specifically who he could get to climb it with him and what the present weather there might be. Joe had it on good authority that it just snowed on Assiniboine and now would not be a good time.

"I fucked up," Fred assured us, "I really fucked up." Earlier in the season he had a partner (or partners), but timing was wrong for Fred who really fucked up and didn't go and now the partner(s) couldn't go and the weather wasn't good. Maybe he should go to Tuolumne and do Lucky Streaks, and what did we think?

I said the weather in Tuolumne had a better chance of being good than at Assiniboine. I didn't say that for Fred to have any chance of getting up either Assiniboine, the Matterhorn of the Rockies, or Lucky Streaks, a four star Tuolumne 5.10d classic, would optimally require an experienced partner or partners 40 to 60 years his junior. Fred knows this better than I do, but such considerations are only part of the larger strategy, like carrying the right size protection for the climb, not taking too heavy a load, and not being afraid to say "I really fucked up" and moving on from it with the intention not to fuck up again. Even the illustrious Fred Beckey at 84 is not going to lead 5.10d or a climb of Assiniboine; but no one else that age is talking or even thinking about it much less plotting to get up either from any point on the rope. Most people are dead before they reach 84. Few of those still standing remain consumed by the passion of their childhood. Of those whose passion is mountain climbing, Fred is the only one I know of who is still climbing, still on the road to another climb, still thinking of the next climb, still talking about women with the enthusiastic lustful libido of an unattached wanderer in his 20s, still true to his original vision and, thereby, himself in action. There is purity to Fred Beckey and his path in life stands, as does Fred himself, as an object lesson in ... purity itself.

Not that the secretive, always on the move, elusive, most prolific climber ever is going to reveal his thinking too precisely, but there were hints that Assiniboine and Lucky Streaks were candidates for the last four spots in his mysterious book to be about North America's 100 best climbs. Joe publishes books for a living and had a more than intellectual mountaineer's curiosity about Fred's book plans. We tried to elicit information, but except for a couple of comments about various (one in particular) "fucking publishers" of Beckey's stellar literary past the most we could get out of him was that a book is in the works. No matter how many times Joe assured him that his information about conditions on Assiniboine was reliable, Beckey brought up the topic at least 20 times. "So, ya think Assiniboine is no good, eh?" he queried.

"No, it just snowed there," Joe repeated.

We reached the turnout next to the highway and were quickly organized and on the short but steep 20 minute (for us) approach to the backside of the Tower. Among my regular climbing partners I am the slowest on approaches and am usually left in the dust of their haste. On this day I took the lead, adapted my pace to match Fred's and was bemused to note that the adjustment was not as noticeable as I might have thought. With his forward lean and ski poles Fred appeared to walk more comfortably uphill than he did on the flats. We moved at a talking pace.

A fine trail up to Gallatin Tower has been constructed from the scree and steep eroding hillside of the approach. "This is a really good trail," Fred observed. "Must've taken a lot of work."

Joe was pleased. The trail was built a few years before by the Southwest Montana Climber's Coalition, of which Joe is Secretary, a member of the BOD and a prime mover and hands-on laborer in SMCC's climbing area trail projects. Joe explained to Fred a little about the Coalition and the trails and pointed out one across the canyon leading up to Sparerib and other good climbs. Yes, all the trails take a lot of work.

As we approached the Tower Fred noted, "Looks like pretty good rock, eh?"

Yes, it's good, we both assured him.

Ten steps later he queried, "So, ya think Assinaboine is no good, eh?"

No, it's no good we both assured him.

"Tuolumne should be better, eh?"

Yes, Tuolumne weather had a better chance of being better.

Joe, hoping to find out if Fred had a publisher in mind, began talking about the perils and rewards of owning his own publishing company, First Ascent Press. Fred didn't say much. I picked up the conversation and commiserated with Joe over the intricacies, facets and unappreciated difficulties of being a publisher.

Joe downplayed the rigors of publishing and the slim margins of error of professional decisions by saying, "Well, it's not exactly rocket science."

Fred immediately responded, "It's not rocket science but it's still work." He quickly steered the conversation away from publishing and into the perils of the evilness of work which interferes with climbing, traveling and other more important aspects of life. Fred Beckey did not become the world's most profuse mountaineer by shirking the often brutal labor required to get up his many climbs. Nor did he do so by embracing any tighter or longer than he might (and, in truth, has) a transitory girl friend in one of the towns along that endless road what stern, upstanding, conservative acolytes of the Wall Street Journal call "the work ethic." Fred's previously published books, including "Mount McKinley," "Cascade Alpine Guide," and "Challenge of the North Cascades" are the work of a meticulous, scholarly researcher, described by Neil Modie in the Seattle Post-Intelligencer as, "...erudite historian, geographer, explorer and author who happens to be a climbing bum."

And we didn't find out anything more about the 100 best climbs in North America.

So it went.

Soon enough we reached the base of the back of Gallatin Tower and the oft guided 5.6 three pitch route. We were quickly harnessed, racked and roped up. Joe, who had climbed the route often, took the first pitch. It went quickly and easily though protection is less than ideal. Joe and I had been curious about how Fred would climb. We were pleased to see that he climbs just fine, just like any good climber half his age, moving with more grace and assurance on vertical rock than he does on horizontal ground. His enjoyment in the moment of the climb is evident and inspiring. Fred is walking, talking, climbing, grimacing proof of the existential dictum often attributed to Jean Paul Sartre: "It's not what you can't do any more; it's what you can do now."

At the first belay we admired the good weather and rock, assured that the climb was going to go well. I took the second lead on pretty good rock and pretty spotty protection. Fred, who did not reach the age of 84 by being comfortable with pretty spotty protection, watched closely. At a point when the answer was obvious and negative he asked, "Got any gear up there?"

Not much, but the climbing wasn't hard and I moved with the delicate knowledge that one falls as far off 5.6 as off 5.14. I was amused, informed and gratified that Fred paid attention to every detail of the climb. Fred Beckey gives us great hope that the aging process need not negate the significance, the meaning or the present moment in action of the physical life. The second pitch ends at the anchors for the second rappel station coming off Gallatin Tower. It is a small ledge fifteen feet below a huge one at the base of the third pitch. Fred led this section between ledges with an aggressive élan unavailable to any other 84 year old in the history of climbing or, for that matter, any other endeavor. That's an admittedly bold statement on behalf of an old climber.

As we were getting ready for the last and hardest pitch Fred asked again about Assiniboine. He received the same answer. I led this last pitch and was happy to find two bolts protecting the crux section. The pitch is rated 5.6, but members of the Dirty Sox Club have earned a deserved reputation among non-Montana climbers for practicing the dark gray, smarmy art of the sandbag, a colloquialism with potential real life consequences. It's a lovely pitch, but one wouldn't in good conscience put a climber whose limit was 5.6 upon it. The top of the tower offers a beautiful view of the canyon. It was a crisp, clear day and a pleasure to be where we were, doing what we were doing. Good fun. Good health. Good companions. Good landscape.

Joe came next so he could take photos of Fred, and he got some beauties, particularly one of Fred's gnarled old hands grasping a hold in just the right way. Fred cruised the last pitch and we sat on top taking in the sights—the Gallatin River, the canyon, the climbs across the river, the highway with its snarl of trucks and automobiles and frustrated drivers, one small slice of the great, vibrant, crazy landscape of western America. We talked about the world and about American politics as viewed from the top of Gallatin Tower. Fred was born in Germany in 1923 and immigrated to America as a child. He is as disturbed, baffled, pissed off and alarmed as every other honest, clear thinking, compassionate American by the war in Iraq and those people in high and low stations who brought it to the world on our dime and moral standing; but Fred has a longer view, a more powerful scope than most, one, I assume, that is both cause and consequence of maintaining the passion of youth.

We rappelled to the bottom for a late lunch. We each had brought our own victuals, but Fred's was the most memorable—a five day old turkey sandwich that came from his girl friend who had gotten it from an airline that bungled her flight to Bozeman to meet Fred and caused her to overnight somewhere but provided her with a free lunch that she passed on to Fred who had been saving it. He offered part of it to us. "It's really good," he said, putting forward a worn white roll with white turkey and white mayonnaise, but I am a vegetarian and refusing his generosity was easy. Joe the carnivore didn't get off so easily, but his own food sufficed.

We offered Fred another climb. He replied that we should go ahead but that his back was sore. He looked tired. What 84 year old would not? So we packed up and returned to the car and went back down the canyon to Davy's. We weren't yet ready to call it a day and say goodbye, so Fred jumped in his Subaru wagon with the crunched-in front and we met a couple of miles down the road at Mama Mac's, our favorite coffee/ food spot in Gallatin Gateway, also known as Four Corners, the busy intersection of Highways 191 and 84, where Fred bought me carrot cake and coffee with a crisp $20 bill from his wallet. "In a hundred years we won't have any use for this stuff," he announced with a smile, plopping the bill on the counter. "We might as well use it up while we can."

One hundred years????

Fred picked up a small stack of Mama Mac's business cards, which he will use as his own business cards by writing his pertinent information on the back and passing them out. It's just one of Fred's personal environmentally sensitive practices.

The carrot cake was wonderful. While we ate Fred pulled out a well used Fed Ex envelope from which he extracted a printed description of a candidate for his 100 best climbs, one in Arizona I'd never heard about. We read the description and it looks good. We talked about climbing in Arizona, about Assiniboine, Tuolumne, the road, the new library in Bozeman where Fred wanted to do some research. And then Joe and I had to go. Fred announced he'd stay in Mama Mac's a bit longer. He seemed to be pondering whether he was going to go to the library for research, back to Davy's, to Assiniboine, to Tuolumne, to Seattle, or toward some other unknown (to us) destination or peak along a road that in a hundred years will seem as exotic to those who read about it as the travels of Marco Polo are to us. Whatever the details and adventures of that road, past and future, it is of a kind and traveled in the spirit of Polo, Magellan, Stanley, Amundsen, Shackleton, Thesiger, Shipton, Tilman and David-Neel. Joe and I had more mundane duties to attend to and we said our good-byes and left Fred alone at the table looking like a tired 84 year old taking a well deserved, much appreciated break.

Outside, before we got in the car, Joe said, "Somehow, it doesn't seem right to just leave him sitting there alone."

"He's a big boy," I replied, "and he's been on the road a long time. Fred's just fine, Joe, Fred's just fine."

CHAPTER SIXTEEN

Glimpses of Pratt

1939 – 2000

THAILAND 2000

Chuck Pratt lay down and went to sleep and never woke up. It is impossible to know what it is to die until we do and none of us will ever experience another man's death, but from this side of things Pratt's doesn't sound so bad. He made even that final, most difficult move of life with an effortless grace and quiet mystery that touched everyone who knew him. Three days before he died he wrote these words to a friend: "I haven't felt this happy since I got out of the army 40 years ago.... Did you know a man can die of pleasure overload?" As I wrote via e mail to one of Chuck's friends a couple of days after he died: The thing we need to ponder is this: What was Chuck dreaming when he checked out?

YOSEMITE 1968-1974

By the time I arrived in Yosemite in 1968 as a novice climber, Chuck was an established master of big wall and hard technical rock climbing, regarded by cognoscenti with a respect verging on reverence. I watched him climb but did not know enough to realize what I was seeing. He free climbed like a magician, a man born to vertical stone, comfortable where others struggled. There was another reason Chuck's pains were so difficult to perceive, a reason many in the climbing world completely overlooked when thinking about, relating to and (alas) judging Chuck Pratt. It was most aptly summed up by Joe McKeown who observed after Chuck's death that he was "Certainly the most humble and creative of the old gang." He was also deeply intelligent, wildly talented and inherently shy.

It was Pratt who first strung a rope between trees in Camp 4 and walked it to practice balance. And Pratt rode a unicycle and juggled to hone coordination and concentration, balance and gracefulness. He made a discipline and game of finesse as John Bachar and other later Yosemite climbers would do with power and endurance. And he was one of the few climbers then or now with the patience and concentration to detail to climb 5.2 with the same craft and precise attention with which he climbed 5.10 or 5.11. Such care and respect verging on reverence for what he was doing set Chuck apart from his contemporaries in more ways than in the complex convergence of qualities, skills and deeds that constitute a climbing reputation. And he wasn't fooled for a second by those old charlatans, fortune, fame, and worldly ambition, or tempted by the psychic violence that is the path of upwardly mobile social respectability. Above all, Chuck Pratt was his own man.

He is quoted as having said in 1965: "I feel that my enemy is anyone who would, given the power to do so, restrict individual liberty, and this includes all officials, law officers, army sergeants, communists, Catholics and the House Un-American Activities Committee. Of course, I am prejudiced, but I cannot imagine a sport other than climbing which offers such a complete and fulfilling expression of individuality. And I will not give it up nor even slow down, not for man, nor woman, nor wife, nor God."

Chuck was his own man.

Yosemite at Night

In general, it is fair to say that the Yosemite/Berkeley climbing scene of the 1960s and 70s explored and indulged in mind/mood/emotion altering chemicals with at least as much fervor as it explored and expanded the climbing possibilities of the fine rock walls of the valley. Climbers' parties in Yosemite were as wild and frenzied and fun (i.e. interesting) as any I've ever known, and I knew a lot of them. To see climbing legends on their knees in the dirt of Camp 4 howling at the moon or at the park rangers sent over to quiet things down usually elicited one of two responses among the uninitiated: change camps or do a little howling yourself. With the same quiet intensity he brought to rock climbing, Pratt immersed himself into whatever party was at hand. In the way such things tend to evolve for some people, in later years Chuck was at times a one-man party all his own. His demons were always there, kept in marginal control most of the time with skepticism merging into cynicism, a careful thoroughness to order and restraint in those matters that he could control (like climbing and the precise disposition of each stick of firewood outside his cabin on Guides Hill), and, of course, keeping busy with chores and work. Drugs were a necessary release, but they also released the demons. Alcohol in the form of beer was his drug of choice to the end.

LOVERS LEAP 1970

Except for guiding together in the Tetons, I climbed only once with Chuck. He showed up at Lovers Leap after driving across the desert from somewhere....the southwest or the Tetons most likely. He had rolled a car along the way but survived with only a sprained or dislocated left thumb which hung uselessly and could not close with the first finger. Still, he wanted to climb so we did The Line, a classic three-pitch route neither of us had done before. He led the first and hardest pitch with a hand and a half, and whether his impairment hindered or pained him could not be discerned, and he did not dwell on the pain or inconvenience or whatever adaptations he needed to make. The Line was a hard route of that time, and it was the first time I was able to see the creativity McKeown later noted. Because of his injury I expected him to struggle. When he did not, I was made aware of Pratt's amazing power of focus which guided his life and allowed him to tap deeper and climb higher than others. Climbing The Line with Pratt was an education in climbing as something beyond and quite different from brutal struggle, though, when necessary, Pratt struggled with the best. I remember that route as a turning point in my own climbing and from that day on I knew Chuck to be graceful and gracious, funny and serious, and a man who both knew what he was doing and what he was about.

Pratt was the most creative and humble of his peers. About the time we climbed The Line he also came up with a typically wry definition of the greatest climber in the world as "Someone who solos a difficult new route from the bottom of the Grand Canyon to the rim at night, and never tells anyone about it." Only now that Pratt is gone does it occur to me that he may have done just that on one of his many trips to the Southwest. It is exactly the way in which Pratt would have obliquely referred to his own talent and to having done something that no one else would or could do. More, it amuses me to think that he might have done it as much as it pleases me to contemplate his personal satisfaction and pleasure in guarding such a secret treasure. It would be very much like him to measure up to his own definition of the greatest climber in the world, and never tell anyone about it.

Women

Well, yes, of course. Always. Pratt loved (he also lusted after) women in general and a special few in particular. Pratt was humble and shy, but he was a hedonist with a heart at heart and women loved him for it. He was also interesting as hell and interested as well.

The Tetons 1993-2000

As an Exum guide fortunate enough to spend summers living on Guides Hill at Lupine Meadow beneath the east face of Teewinot, I was Pratt's neighbor for part of each year. From that time I offer a few word portraits of Pratt, perhaps something in prose like the hundreds of photographs he took in the last years of every and any woman willing to pose for his camera, his eye, his imagination and fantasies.

Guiding a group of adolescents up Cube Point early in the season we had to cross a section of snow. I fixed a rope and we got our charges across the snow with no incidents. Pratt, dressed in his trademark balaclava, hated snow, cold, ice and winter with a neurotic fury that was amusing to others but which was painfully serious to him. He came across last with characteristic precision and a scowl on his face. I grinned at him, and he knew why. "I can't believe we're bringing these poor, innocent children here and actually teaching them to walk on this ... stuff", he said, indicating the steps cut in the snow. "I always avoid it and consider stepping in it the same way I would consider stepping in radioactive dog shit. We've sunk so low in life that we're making our living teaching innocent children to walk upon radioactive dog shit."

The Pratt cabin at Lupine Meadow was a marvel of order in the small community of Exum guides whose places of residence, for the most part, appeared more disorderly than Chuck's, though in general they were not. His firewood, stacked around the cabin with the precision of considered thought to each piece, looked more the work of a master stone mason than a readily available source of fuel. The wooden clothes pins on his clothes line were impregnated with linseed oil and looked like small pieces of fine woodwork made by a patient craftsman. It always seemed to me that, for Pratt, every stick of wood in its exact place, every clothes pin made to last, every move made precisely right, helped keep the demons at bay. When he couldn't hold them off, he all too often closed the door to his cabin behind him and drank in privacy, just alcohol and Chuck and their private demons.

I sometimes talked with Chuck about the things of our lives ... Yosemite days and people, writing (Chuck's few efforts as a writer are among the best climbing literature I know. He once explained why there isn't more: "Writing about climbing is boring. I would rather go climbing."), women (of course), guiding (we seldom spoke of climbing), the humor (because laughter is preferable to tears) to be found in the cornucopia of man's follies, the weather (on cold mornings the balaclava-clad Pratt loved to point out that global warming had to be a myth, a conspiracy by environmentalists and other wackos, among whom he included me), and Thailand (his favorite topic). The Exum community and Guides Hill was his home and his extended family, but his heart was in Thailand.

Chuck behind the wheel of his vintage and unmistakable white/gray and then green Volkswagen squareback on the road between Dornans and Lupine Meadow. He was a study in concentration on the return drive from Dornans, as safe and thoughtful and attentive as any man has ever been in the long, sad, unsafe history of drinking and driving. He was certainly less a threat to himself and his fellow man than half the tourists driving that stretch of road looking for elk and antelope and the occasional moose. I would not hesitate to take my chances on the road with Pratt in the bag any day rather than with the average tourist on the loose and intoxicated by his one week a year of vacation, demented by a momentary view of the unrestricted freedom Pratt aspired to, unfocused by a glimpse of a world not delineated by officials, officers, ideologies, priests and politicians and the economic interests they serve.

In 1998, for various and sound reasons, Chuck made the decision not to drink at all during the guiding season from June to September. This was a sudden, not a long thought out decision. It was a cold turkey determination, a life changing resolution that, in Chuck's case, made a solo climb up a new route out of the Grand Canyon at night seem, in comparison, as easy as driving to Dornans. Everybody on Guides Hill watched Chuck to see whether his resolve would crack, but those of us who had been intimate with obstinate chemical excess and dependency and with the equally difficult, uncompromising, cold-hearted cold turkey watched with the particular interest of the experienced. He never flinched. With the same unqualified intensity he brought to his climbing, Chuck looked the cold turkey in the eye and did not blink. For the last three years of his guiding life he did not drink during the season, though the rest of the year was another story. But our hearts dropped the first time he came back to his cabin from Dornans with a brown paper bag under his arm that looked the size and shape to hold two six packs. Sometime later he came out of his cabin holding a bottle of non-alcoholic beer. I think he did it to relish the effect as much as to enjoy the taste of bogus beer. The recently retired serious drinker suddenly finds an abundance of time and energy in his life that he has forgotten existed. One of the things Chuck did with that time and energy the first summer was to split wood each evening. Cords of rounds became stacks of the most meticulously split and arranged firewood in the history of Guides

Hill. I found myself some evenings just watching Pratt split firewood because it was beautiful to see. He split wood with an ax on a tree-round chopping block. He swung his ax with grace and a respect for minimalist efficiency that I saw as a reverence for finesse. It was masterful work and I will never forget the sight of Chuck Pratt splitting wood with complete focus and all his being. Several of us on Guides Hill are students of Zen Buddhism, and watching Chuck in the evenings always brought to mind the Zen maxim "Chop wood, carry water," pointing the Zen practitioner toward each moment and task with complete focus.

Pratt could have been a fine writer, but it bored him. He would have made a great student of Zen, but he didn't need it. As it was, Chuck Pratt just might have been the greatest climber in the world by his own definition, and he was definitely one of them by anyone's definition. I'm glad he was here. I'm sorry he is gone. I wonder what he was dreaming when he checked out.

PART THREE

Climbing Reflections

A prusik knot   *photo Lito Tejada-Flores*

CHAPTER SEVENTEEN

The Prusik

THE PRUSIK IS A LOOP OF PERLON CORD, or webbing, that is wrapped around a climbing rope in a "lark's foot" and then fed through its own loop two or three times. Three is best. The Prusik must be of a smaller diameter material than the climbing rope. When weighted it will bind and stop anyone attached to it from going anywhere until it is loosened. For this reason it is imperative that the climber always keeps the Prusik attached closer than arm's length to the harness. (I attach mine above the rappel device and to the front of the harness, but there are other methods.) Having a locked Prusik higher than you can reach on a rappel can be a real nuisance. But there are those unexpected times in climbing when not going anywhere, especially down according to the law of gravity or, for the more sophisticated scientifically minded, Einstein's Theory of ,General Relativity (neither of which will register in the mind or nervous system of a falling climber), is just what the climber wants.

In more than 40 years of climbing the Prusik has never saved my life. With luck and attention to the details of climbing I hope to keep it that way. Like a seat belt or an air bag in a car, the Prusik as a life-saver is a back-up system best left untested, a premise that grew out of a time in American climbing when protection was such that practitioners took seriously the admonition, "don't test the system." The Prusik only has to save your life or keep you from a serious injury once to pay its lifetime's way as an invaluable piece of gear on your harness. I never put on my climbing harness without a Prusik on it. I have at least one good friend, Peter Lev, who is alive today only because he was using a Prusik when he needed it. Peter was coming off Dhaulaghiri in a storm when an iced fixed rope came undone from its bottom anchor and only his Prusik kept him from rappelling off the end of the rope. I know some other dead and injured climbers who would have avoided their mishaps had they been using a Prusik.

Many times during those years the Prusik has been a utilitarian treasure on the crags, perhaps even a life saver. There are many useful object lesson stories about climbers using and not using the Prusik, but the point for climbing gear heads is that the Prusik is versatile, light, functional, easy to use, cheap, and invaluable in the moment and circumstance it is needed. Properly used, it will keep a climber from rappelling off the end of the rope, stop him or her immediately if the rappelling climber goes unconscious from a bonk or a rock on the head, fatigue, excitement or spaciness. If the rappel device fails or is improperly attached or used, the rope icy, wet or otherwise not providing enough friction for control, a Prusik will help get the climber home for dinner.

When ascending fixed lines, placing a Prusik between the two ascenders is a good practice, as, of course, is making sure the climber is attached to both ascenders. A few years ago a veteran Yosemite climber fell out of his aid slings and lost his grip on his ascenders while jugging fixed ropes on El Capitan. He was not tied into his aiders, his ascenders or the fixed rope and would have fallen to his death if he had not inadvertently and with a fool's luck become tangled in the fixed line on the way down. After a complicated rescue it was discovered that the fallen climber was not seriously injured, was surly, belligerent, ungrateful to his rescuers and, it was later determined, had been partying all night and had launched himself in the early morning hours upon the beautiful granite of El Cap while still thoroughly in the bag. A Prusik (or 8 hours of sleep, clipping into his ascenders, better judgment and/or more respect) might have saved this cavalier climber, to say nothing of his rescuers, a lot of trouble.

In a pinch (a tight one), a Prusik can be used as a self belay device either on a fixed rope or even if you had to climb and belay yourself out of one of those places you'd rather not be but which do exist and every climber finds from time to time. With two Prusiks and a few slings one can ascend any fixed rope, and before the development of mechanical ascenders that is how fixed ropes were climbed. It is also a handy device for hauling.

The Prusik I use is made of three and a half to four feet of 6 to 8 mm perlon cord with the ends tied together with a water knot. It is the least expensive, lightest, easiest to use (it can be put on with one hand) and, on those occasions when needed, the most valuable piece of gear a climber carries.

Prusik is sometimes spelled Prussick, Prussic or Prussik, but since it was invented by Austrian mountaineer Dr. Karl Prusik and first featured in a 1931 Austrian climbing manual with that spelling I prefer Prusik.

CHAPTER EIGHTEEN

The Snaz

...and I dig all you cats out there whippin' and whalin' and jumpin' up and down and suckin' up that fine juice, and pattin' each other on the back and tellin' each other who the greatest cat in the woild is. Mr. Malenkoff, Mr. Dalenkoff, Mr. Eisenhower, Woozinweezin, Weisenwoozer, and Mr. Woodhill and Mr. Beechhill and Mr. Churchhill and all them Hills, they gonna get it straight. If they can't straighten it they know a cat that knows a cat that's gonna get it straight. Well, I'm gonna put a cat on you was the sweetest, gonist, wailinest cat that ever stomped on this sweet swingin' sphere. And they call this here cat...the Nazz, that was the cat's name. He was a carpenter kitty. Now the Nazz was the kind of a cat that come on so wild, and so sweet, and so strong and so with it, that when he laid it— WHAM—it stayed there...

    —The great hipster comedian Lord Richard Buckley
      on the Nazz, the man from Nazareth, known
      among the less hip as Jesus Christ

AND ON AUGUST 4, 1964 Mort Hempel and Yvon Chouinard, two of the sweetest, gonist, wailinest climber cats that ever had faith that a hundred or so feet of rope tied into a tiny Swami belt would save them from the inevitable fall went into Death Canyon in the wilderness of Wyoming's Teton Range. And there they saw Cathedral Rock rising up above into the heavens and a line up that rock so straight and fine it caused them to commence whippin' and wailin' and jumpin' up and down and suckin' up that fine juice, and pattin' each other on the back. With the faith that ends fear they straight away stomped up that nine pitch 5.9 Grade IV sweet swingin' route that was so wild, so sweet, so strong, so with it that when they laid it after a few hours of tapping bongs and pitons into the Cathedral to protect them from their sins—WHAM—it stayed there as a classic and one of the most popular climbs in the Tetons.

Though they thought it was a snazzy route, they named it for the Nazz and called it The Snaz.

CHAPTER NINETEEN

What's at the Root of the Name of the Route

Proper names are poetry in the raw. Like all poetry they are untranslatable.
—W.H Auden

A proper name is a word that answers the purpose of showing what thing it is that we are talking about, but not of telling anything about it.
—John Stuart Mill

IT IS A SIGNIFICANT MATTER to bestow a name, upon a person, place, thing, entity, or climbing route whether done in reverence, mockery, esteem, silliness, as a pun or insider joke, factual geographic description, or cultural statement. There are consequences and sometimes pertinent information about a climbing route contained in its name. There is always information contained in a route's name about the thinking, culture or mind-set of him, her, or those who conferred it. As such, the name of a climbing route is, in my view, a too-little noted and largely unappreciated aspect of the history, culture and present moment of the experience of climbing. There is a saying that words have meaning but names have power.

Both the Muir and Salathe Walls on Yosemite's El Capitan were named in honor of the two Johns, John Muir and John Salathe, icons of Yosemite and the values of reverence for the natural world and simple life by which they lived. The names themselves, the Muir Wall and the Salathe Wall, have raised both the climbing and larger worlds' consciousness about the lives of those men and what they represented in ways that cannot be measured but are appreciated. It is unlikely that the people who named those routes would have chosen Rockefeller Wall, Peabody Wall, Rothschild Wall, or Roosevelt Wall, even though Theodore Roosevelt was crucial to establishing the National Park System. If they had honored America's robber barons instead of its lovers of nature, a good argument could be made that it would have changed the flavor of Yosemite (and thereby American) climbing, and without question it would have altered the nomenclature of subsequent climbing routes. The very nature (sic) of Camp 4 dirtbag climbers' campfire conversations and rants would have been completely changed in unimaginable ways by contemplating or describing the Peabody Wall rather than the Muir Wall, or the Roosevelt Wall instead of the Salathe Wall, even if referring to the same piece of stone.

Royal Robbins, Tom Frost and Chuck Pratt made the first ascent of the Salathe Wall in 1961 and named it, in Robbins' words, "...to honor our beloved predecessor." According to T.M. Herbert, at the time Salathe was as big a name in the climbing community as Robbins' and the name was meant to describe "the whole damned wall" left of the Nose and not just a route. It was only the 2nd route up El Capitan after the Nose route and it broke new ground in both style of Yosemite climbing and naming of routes, consistent with Robbins' entire career as America's preeminent rock climber of his time. "A good name for a climb is a sort of short poem," Robbins replied to an inquiry about naming the Salathe Wall, and so it is.

Yvon Chouinard and Herbert did the first ascent of what they named the Muir Wall in 1965. It was the 4th route on El Cap. Herbert, who when he lived in Berkeley used to visit Muir's home and museum in Martinez, said Muir was "a hero of nature and conservation" and so far ahead of his time in the environmental movement that they wanted to recognize him. It is worth mentioning here that Chouinard and his company Patagonia are today (2008) at the forefront of environmental activism and consciousness raising in America. An interesting aside is that Robbins noted he would have named it the "John Muir Route," but it was not his to name.

Other El Cap route names are simple geographic descriptions: West Face, West Buttress, The Nose, East Buttress, and The East Ledges Descent.

These names do not require much elaboration or investigation to understand the intention of those who named them.

Other El Cap names are not so easily grasped by the uninitiated to the culture and the time of the people who bestowed the names: Tangerine Trip, The Central Scrutinizer, Grape Race, Magic Mushroom, Bermuda Dunes, and Realm of the Flying Monkey. And that's just one rock in one valley in one state, though it is the iconic rock of American climbing. Every climber has his and her own realm of routes climbed and, in many cases, named in various areas all over the world. Every climbing guide book contains a wide and wild range of names of routes from the bizarre to the boring, from inspired to offensive (to somebody), from the subtle to in-your-face, from humorous to macabre. And often themes run through the names of an area's climbing routes, not all of them as wholesome as honoring Muir and Salathe, but each of them affecting the consciousness and conversation of every climber's campfire sermons and rants about that climb.

Idaho's City of Rocks has Decadent Wall with a range of names guaranteed to offend or at least bring a blush to somebody recognizing explicit human organs and intimacy, chauvinism and crassness, or homage to past relationships. The National Organization for Women took some hostile interest in the sexist flavor of Decadent Wall and some names were provocative enough that they were eventually changed. Dave Bingham's latest guide book to the City includes this caveat: "In the early 80s Utah climber Jay Goodwin coined the 'decadent' theme, using sexually-oriented names for about a dozen climbs. I decided to omit some names because they are idiotic and were not given by the first ascentionists." So much for the first amendment. The new, censored/altered City of Rocks guidebook lists these names: Dykes on Harleys, Carol's Crack, Divine Decedance, Flesh for Fantasy, Adolescent Homosapien, FDC, Bestiality, Kibbles and Bits, Sex, Drugs & Rock & Roll, Life Without

Sex, Estrogen Imbalance, Sexual Dysfunction, Frigidity, Testosterone Test, Impotence, Stiff Vegetables, Box Lunch, Just Hold Still, Self Abuse, and Shaved in the Shape of a Heart. A bit of raucous imagination and licentious license will allow the reader to trace Bingham's somewhat staid names back to the original 'idiotic' ones. For those of a less decadent droop of mind, the original guide book lists these routes on Decadent Wall: Dikes on Harleys, Watersports, Submission, Carol's Crack, Flesh for Fantasy, Devine Decadence, Adolescent Homo, FDC (which is reported to stand for Fucking Dead Cows), Beastiality, Rancid Virgins, Dimples and Tits, Nipples and Clits, Preteen Sex, Abortion on Parade, Life Without Sex, Estrogen Imbalance, Sexual Dysfunction, Frigidity, Testosterone Test, Impotence, Stiff Vegetables, Box Lunch, Just Hold Still, Self Abuse, and Shaved in the Shape of a Heart. (A few weeks ago I encountered Goodwin having dinner in Almo, the closest community to the City of Rocks. He was enjoying looking through the charming homework papers and drawings of his six year old daughter, and I neglected to solicit his thoughts about the transformation of names of Decadent Wall routes or whether he thought his daughter would better appreciate Dad's original names or Bingham's tidied up ones.)

The drug culture has made a significant impact on American climbing and expanded its possibilities and standards in ways both subtle and obvious, including the naming of routes. It continues to do so. The double-entendre in the name of the group of climbers who called themselves The Stone Masters is one of my favorites, and their contribution to pushing the limits of climbing is certainly mind-expanding. Among the many well known routes with drug inspired names (and, perhaps, first ascents) are Left, Right and Middle Peyote Cracks in Joshua Tree, Columbian Crack, and White Line Fever at the City of Rocks, Tangerine Trip, Mescalito, Magic Mushroom and Pyschedelic Shack in Yosemite, and Drug Nasty (a.k.a. Dean's Dream), Lethal Dose, Panama Red, Cocaine Crack ,and Powder up the Nose at Smith Rocks. And the popular Tuolumne route Oz is not named after the famous wizard of, but rather is the accepted abbreviation for ounce. Oz is on Drug Dome and connects to Gram Traverse.

Like every climber, I have my own realm of experience, knowledge and perspective concerning the naming of climbing routes. Some of it is included here because I believe my own experience is not so different from that of other climbers, and if history matters (and I think it does) then clarifying history is crucial. If a name has power, then the more one understands about the name the more power it has and the more satisfying the experience of doing the climb. Climbers name routes for different reasons and to contribute different legacies to the world of climbing.

At one time we were taken with naming routes according to a message hidden within the given title. For instance, in 1972 Sibylle Hechtel and I named a route on Mt. Mitchell in the Wind River Range "Ecclesiastes." Joe Kelsey, who might be called the John Muir of the Wind River Range, was not amused, pleased or in favor of the name because of the precedent it might set. But neither Sibylle (I believe) nor I are Bible students or, at least in my case, even Christian. We named it because of the great line in Ecclesiastes, "It is all emptiness and chasing the wind," an apt description of climbing itself and, one might say, much else in life. The author of Ecclesiastes obviously thought so. The name of the route had nothing to do with Bible thumping or Christian theology, though it did (and does) pay homage to the wisdom of it being all emptiness and chasing the wind. The name stuck in certain circles but so far as I know it has never been included in a guide book by its proper name.

A year earlier Chris Vandiver and I named a route on Lembert Dome in Tuolumne Meadows Truckin' Drive. It is next to the older route Rawl Drive, named after the Rawl drill which was used in the early days of placing bolts (and which was used in the placing of the original bolts on both routes). Truckin' Drive was named after the Grateful Dead song "Truckin'" and particularly for the famous verse:

Sometimes the light's all shinin' on me;
Other times, I can barely see.
Lately it occurs to me...
What a long, strange trip it's been.

In the guide books Truckin' Drive is misnamed Truck 'N Drive, a misnomer that matters mostly to those who named the route and to those curious about the significance of the name and of the long, strange trip between the two very different names with totally different meanings and possible connotations. A truck and truckin' are as different as a pair of pants and pantin'.

That same Tuolumne summer of 1971 Wayne Merry and I named a route on Daff Dome "El Condor Pasa" from the then popular song of that name by Simon and Garfunkle on their album "Bridge Over Troubled Water," and, more specifically, the line written by Paul Simon and Jorge Milderberg, "I'd rather be a hammer than a nail." The music for this lovely song was actually written in 1913 by the Peruvian Daniel Alomia Robles. Wayne was on lead and not very happy about his pro and his run out when he yelled with great relief that he'd found a chicken head. After he tied it off and clipped in he said that it wasn't a chicken head, it was a condor head. The condor allowed us to pass and we would rather be hammer than nail, and as with Truckin' Drive there is much lost in the Tuolumne guide books that call the route El Condor instead of the original El Condor Pasa.

There are undoubtedly names of other routes that have gradually and perhaps inadvertently, or, in cases like Decadent Wall, suddenly morphed into something quite different from what the original name intended. Poetry in the raw turned to poetry dressed in a mistake or the censor's morality or good citizen's sense of good taste.

There is a rock formation at the City of Rocks that used to be called Hershey's Kiss because its top resembled one. On the left side of its west face is a 5.12 three star overhanging jam crack route. Tony Yaniro is credited by Bingham as doing the first ascent of this fine route, but Stan Caldwell disputes this. According to Caldwell, Yaniro started the route but couldn't complete it and Caldwell found the key to the route in a hidden hold at the crux that one 'ought to see' in order to get through. Through a process that can be imagined but probably never completely tracked, both the rock formation and its best route are now known as Odyssey, though for personal reasons my favorite routes and route names there are Driving at Night and Just Another Mormon on Drugs.

Yosemite's Crack of Doom was first climbed and aptly named by Pratt in 1961. This led to another intimidating route of a different flavor being named Crack of Despair soon after and even another Crack of Doom named by George Lowe at the City of Rocks. These names are poetry eliciting the feeling of beginning such routes and, of course, they inspire puns. Many years and several states away in Colorado's Unaweep Canyon is a far easier route named Crack of Don, though I have been unable to find out anything about Don.

Every guide book and even climbing areas without them contain names to suit every taste—intriguing, offensive, inspiring, descriptive, confusing, dumb, clever, incomprehensible and sappy. A guide to Oregon's Smith Rocks includes Vomit Launch, Victory of the Proletarian People's Ambion Arete, Virgin Slayer, Shark-infested Waters, Silly Boy, Chairman Mao's Little Red Book, Walking While Intoxicated, and Darkness at Noon.

Climbers in Utah's Wasatch Range have named routes Satan's Corner, St. Alphonso's Pancake Breakfast, Nipple Remover, Shadow of Death and Mind Blow. There is also a plethora of religious themed names including Final Prayer Variation, Garden of Eden, Holy Grail, Judas Priest, Lazarus, Missionary Jam, The Rosary, and Celestial Ascension.

The point is that every route has a name (except, of course, the few orphaned, nameless ones looking for adoption or at least discovery), and a name has significance, power, history, personality, thoughtfulness, and thoughtlessness. Understanding or at least contemplating both the significance and the power in the name of a route adds to the meaning and experience, even the poetry, of doing the climb. Check it out next time you do a climb. Discover the stone poetry at the root of the name of the route.

The North Face of Everest from the Rongbuk Monastery.   photo Dick Dorworth

CHAPTER TWENTY

The Blue Sheep at Rongbuk

OUR LAST MORNING AT RONGBUK MONASTERY was emotional with farewell to a unique and spectacular place and time. It was 1981 and we were among the first westerners to visit the Rongbuk Valley under the massive north face of Everest since China began its experiment with openness to the rest of the world.

At 16, 500 feet elevation the monastery had been the highest on Earth, the home of some 300 Tibetan Buddhist monks. Rongbuk means "valley of caves" and long before Buddhism arrived from India followers of Tibet's ancient Bon religion sought out these caves for spiritual quests. The landscape was as stark as it was beautiful, steeped in the energy and tradition of spiritual aspiration and the highest of human mountaineering ambition.

We were 13 Americans, most of them old friends of mine from Nevada; two Canadians; and three Chinese escorts. I was leader of this commercial trek to see Tibet and its people and to visit the north side of Everest where our permit allowed us to reach an elevation of 18,000 feet. Since our Chinese guardsmen went no higher than the monastery where the trucks that had driven us across Tibet from Lhasa deposited them, we were free to do as we pleased and were able above 16,500. That wasn't much in terms of elevation gain, though a few of us managed to wander up to around 20,000, but it was huge in terms of experience, perspective and appreciation of one of the most stunning and moving places on earth. None of us wanted to leave that last morning. All of us were disgusted and angry with the Chinese because of what China had done and was doing (and is still doing) to Tibet and its people. Everyone in our group was enchanted with and filled with admiration and concern for the people and countryside of Tibet.

We had learned that Tibet bore a striking physical resemblance to Nevada and that its people were cheerful, open, curious and deeply religious. They won our hearts with their shy friendliness. The land, its creatures, people and traditions had been subjugated and brutalized by the army of the People's Republic of China, the invader and unwelcome occupier of Tibet, a pugnacious gang of thugs in a temple.

The once exquisite Rongbuk monastery lay in ruins, shelled and reduced to rubble by the Chinese military which might more accurately be described as the army of the Pugnacious Republic of Thuggery. Of the more than 2500 Tibetan monasteries in existence when the Chinese invaded in 1951 less than 10 were intact 30 years later. In the jumbled remains of Rongbuk were thousands of shattered examples of Buddhist art, mani stones and frescoes, the work of centuries by patient, skilled and devoted monks, sad glimpses of another time, poignant reminders of impermanence.

Tibet's mystery and the allure of Everest had been our enticement, but the dignity and strength of Tibetans in the face of Chinese brutality and desecration of Tibet's culture and landscape were our memories. Tibetans know how to smile, though life has never been easy. The Chinese invasion only made it harder, as always happens when barbarity invades compassion, including the deaths of more than 1.2 million Tibetans and the additional deaths by torture of some 26,000, many of them Buddhist monks and nuns. The snow-covered Himalaya loom over sparse, green valleys from which efficient people had long nurtured a living from infertile soil and climate with the tools of labor, intelligence and faith. Our group of tourists viewed both people and landscape with awe. Our Chinese hosts viewed and treated them with disdain.

We had seen a few hares, ducks, geese, a condor-like lammergeyer and various other birds and domesticated animals during our journey, but there was a notable scarcity of wildlife in Tibet. We deduced that this eerie paucity of life in a vast land was related to the conduct of our Chinese escorts. Every time a wild creature appeared, out came the pistols, shotguns and rifles. They were poor shots, though an occasional unlucky hare and pigeon were killed. The most enthusiastic killer ('hunter' is the wrong word as it implies deliberation and connection to the natural world) was Tong, our cook, who claimed to be hunting food for us. This was untrue, as none of Tong's kills were ever cleaned, much less cooked and eaten. Tong killed for the thrill and, perhaps, for the small sense of control in a life over which he had little control; but Tong had his story and stuck to it.

Tong was a handsome, athletic fellow with an abundance of malevolent energy that he channeled into suspicious resentment toward our party. But he was no cook, as three weeks of his mostly inedible meals proved. We learned that he had come to Tibet with the Chinese army. He married a Tibetan woman and had a family in Lhasa, but he treated the native people with angry condescension and an always visibly implied threat of violence. His profession was coaching soccer and he looked every bit the part of a tough, unflinching Asian warrior/athlete. I often thought that if I had known Tong in the context of coaching soccer we could have found some common ground and trust. But Tong had violated some stricture of Communist life and had been stripped of his job. Cooking for the enemy was his society's method of instilling humility into his proud soldier/athlete soul and bending him to its will. Such upheaval is common in Communist China. At that time it was not unusual for doctors, engineers and scientists to spend some of the best, most productive years of their lives as field hands and miners to keep them from thinking too deeply or independently. Doubting dogma and questioning authority are not permitted in China. The result in Tong's case was a deeply resentful and hopelessly inept cook who fought back by sabotaging our own social/political system and our physical ones in every way possible. Each member of our group lost between five and 20 pounds during our time together.

There wasn't much about Tong to like, but if he could not fight without dire and possibly fatal consequences the system that would make of him a cook for the hated westerners, he would and did fight us with every tool at his disposal. He took pride in letting us know he did not need or bow down to us. His government was despicable, his cooking disgusting, his demeanor deplorable, but there was something about his spirit that I admired and that made me laugh (not very often). He was a warrior and he would hold his ground even as that ground diminished, and while he might be defeated and beaten he would never surrender, never be broken. In that he was more like the Tibetans and perhaps his Tibetan wife than he would ever know.

The last morning of our two-week base camp stay at Rongbuk we were all loaded into the "Chinese Liberation Truck" (the Chinese actually named the truck that in honor of the Orwellian deceit that China had 'liberated' Tibet) for the dusty, arduous 500 mile ride on dirt roads back to Lhasa. Emotions were high. My own reluctance to leave Rongbuk was less sentimental than visceral—as if I were leaving home for the first time. We looked with gratefulness, longing and a recognized sense of humility upon Rongbuk and Everest.

Suddenly, a herd of nawa, the graceful, endangered Tibetan blue sheep, magically appeared in the monastery ruins. Two of them jumped up on the remnants of a wall. We knew that blue sheep were in the valley but we had not previously seen them. It was a thrilling farewell sign, an enchanted few moments, a portent, and a time warp in which man and beast were in harmony.

Like Eden, it didn't last long.

Tong, rifle in hand, was out of the cab (Chinese rode in the covered cab; paying guests in the open back) with the speed of a trained soldier. As he raised his weapon to fire an amazing thing happened. Everyone in the back of the truck spontaneously rose in unison and shouted as one voice a warning to the nawa, and, more significantly, a condemnation warning hinting at threat to Tong. We finally had enough of mindless slaughter. A message in sound via the animal chemistry wireless was transmitted to Tong which said that shooting a nawa would start an international incident detrimental to everyone concerned.

Tong lowered his rifle. He looked up at the westerners he so disliked with a look of bewilderment followed by one of slow, cunning realization on his face.

The blue sheep took the hint and vanished as quickly as they had appeared.

We gave Tong a standing ovation, shouting approval and clapping like mad. The freedom to make life or death decisions could not come easily or often to a poor, over-regulated soldier like Tong; and for that reason when they did come he usually chose death. He was stunned by our exuberant show of approval. The enemy applauding. Then Tong shrugged and gave us a wide, handsome, heartfelt smile, the first we had seen from him. He got back in the truck, still smiling.

We drove out of the Rongbuk valley, gazing back at the north face of Everest as long as possible, feeling good.

CHAPTER TWENTY-ONE
Old & New Thoughts on Risk Tolerance

Like many older people I find in recent years that I learn more from those younger than from my peers. I recently gained a new sliver of insight into the matter of risk tolerance from my youngest son, Jason, who lives in Santa Cruz, California and is an avid surfer. Several years ago I heard about Mavericks, the famous, big, dangerous wave an hour north of Santa Cruz. I asked Jason if he knew about and had been to Mavericks. "I don't do that kind of thing, Dad," he replied. As a parent I was understandably relieved. Last year the fine biographical film "Chasing Mavericks," about two Mavericks icons, was released. It is, in my view, a superior film about the human quality of risk tolerance and much more. After I saw it I asked Jason if he had seen it. He knows some of the people portrayed in the film but his busy life as a parent, husband, firefighter, surfer and mountain bike rider had left him no time for the film. But he said something that resonates with lessons for those willing to learn them. He said, "You know, there are only a handful of surfers in the world capable of riding Mavericks, and within that handful there are only a few who want to."

ABOUT 20 YEARS AGO I was talking about the latest casualty of the mountains with a friend, a fellow climbing guide. It is a theme that people who live, work and play in mountains return to all too often. Our discussion that day veered away from the specific most recent death of a climber we knew to all the people we had known who had died in the mountains over the period of our lives. Some of them had been friends, a few close ones. For reasons I've forgotten, we decided that we would search our memories and each make a list of all the people we knew who had died in the mountains. The next day we resumed our conversation with our respective lists which totaled more than 70.

We were both surprised. We should not have been.

There are more names on those lists 20 years later, but neither of us have kept track, nor shall we. People die and are injured every day in the mountains of the world, and it is both easy and practical for mountain people to acknowledge the inevitability and constancy of such events. It is not nearly so painless to move beyond acknowledgement to acceptance. Death and injury, untimely or not, and the questions and diverse answers that arise from them are often neither common nor sensible to everyone, and they are never painless.

Nor are they limited to people and activities of the mountains. They are integral to human life, regardless of where or how lived. There is a usually accepted perception (belief?) that people who engage in such mountainous activities as climbing, skiing, hang gliding, parapenting, kayaking, snowmobiling, snowboarding and the like put themselves at more risk than the general public. A physician I know who views climbing and, I suspect, climbers with jaundiced eye once showed me an article in a medical journal claiming that, statistically, a climber on Denali was more likely to be injured or die than a soldier in combat. I have no idea what data was used to determine that statistic, but that it appeared in a mainstream medical journal illuminates the aforementioned perception. When confronted with such a factual overview of an aspect of life you care about, it is always good to keep in mind the Disraeli adage "There are three kinds of lies: lies, damned lies, and statistics." For me, conflating the unnecessary degradation and horror that war brings to humans with the fundamental beauty, pleasure and spiritual uplifting that mountains instill in them is tasteless in the extreme and a disservice to human understanding of the process of the life, which, inevitably, encompasses death to skier, climber, soldier, housewife and spy alike. I don't know how to determine such a thing, but I suspect that, statistically, physicians who have climbed on Denali lead healthier, happier, and more creative and perhaps even longer lives than do battlefield and more mainstream physicians. And, yes, it is tasteless and an impediment to both understanding and appreciating life to conflate the two, a risk and a choice I am not willing to take. My suspicion is neither a certainty nor a statistic, only an affirmation of the integrity of each person's preference of how to live and of the individual tolerance for risk that choice entails, whether in mountains, cities, battlefields or industrial farms.

I am reminded of Tom Patey's well known verse:

> *Live it up, fill your cup, drown your sorrow*
> *And sow your wild oats while ye may.*
> *For the toothless old tykes of tomorrow,*
> *Were the tigers of yesterday.*

Patey, a fine climber (and doctor), made a simple, human mistake and died in a rappelling accident at the age of 48.

Like all people who have spent a significant amount of their lives engaged in mountainous pursuits, I have dealt with, thought about, observed, engaged in and been affected by the risks and the simple human mistakes inherent to that life. The operational human quality in dealing with those activities I choose to call, for a reason that will soon be clear, 'risk tolerance.' Personally, I am more comfortable (and, I will argue, safer) pursuing a day of any mountainous endeavor with which I am familiar than, say, driving the congested freeways of southern California, walking the streets of many neighborhoods of any large city on earth, dining regularly in the best known fast/junk food restaurants or, needless to say, engaging in violence, whether personally or patriotically inspired. This implies that people are more comfortable (and safer) with the familiar than with the exotic and unrecognizable, but even that does not insulate them from death and injury. Every year more than 30,000 people are killed in car wrecks in America (in 1972 it was 54,000). Every year more than 2500 people are killed in house fires, almost all of them caused by nothing more complicated, risky or unusual than cooking a meal, and more than 13,000 are injured in these fires. In 1978 more than 6,000 people were killed and more than 20,000 injured in house fires. These statistics do not include the firefighters killed and injured trying to save the lives and homes of American people engaged in an activity no more exotic or exposed to risk than cooking dinner for their families. Cooking a meal and driving to the store are not considered high risk activities, at least not statistically, but every day people die and are injured in their pursuit because something went wrong.

And after nearly every accident in the mountains and elsewhere there is a search for answers to why it happened, seeking lessons to be learned to prevent the same mistakes being repeated, sometime assigning blame, always striving to make tidy and comprehensible the complex and often inconceivable. More often than not those searches turn up human error as a primary factor, sometimes incomprehensible error, sometimes completely conceivable. That the lessons are not learned is self-evident. People die and are injured every day in the mountains of the world, and so they will continue to be.

That people often act like sheep and will follow the herd even when knowing they are walking toward the wolves is well established. Detailed accident reports of numerous well-publicized avalanches that resulted in multiple deaths illustrate this. In instances like these, personal tolerance for risk, personal judgment and personal integrity itself are sacrificed (sic) to herd bravura. This dynamic can be observed every day from small groups in every walk of life to entire countries including but not limited to our own. This does not imply that the herd is always wrong just because it is a herd. Sometimes the herd avoids the wolves while one of the sheep goes to them.

For example, four experienced, competent, knowledgeable backcountry skiers were at the top of a steep bowl covered with a foot and a half of fresh snow draining into a long gully with a couple of flat spots along the way. Three of them skied, one at a time, down skier's right of the bowl, into the gully and to the bottom where the snow ran out and they were safe. The fourth skier waited for them before moving left to the center of the bowl and jumping off a fifteen foot cliff to land on the steepest part of the bowl covered with new snow. Naturally, predictably even, the slope avalanched immediately and took the skier for a 1500 foot ride that temporarily buried him in one of the flat spots before a second wave of the slide pushed him along until he wound up at the bottom partially buried, a bit beat up, but very lucky and alive. His friends dug him out and they all went on with their lives. Nice story that easily could have ended not so agreeably. At the end of the official report of this incident was a section titled 'lessons learned.' Not included in those lessons was what seemed to me the obvious one of avoiding jumping off cliffs onto steep, freshly snow loaded terrain. When I queried the writer of the report about this exclusion he replied, "Some people have a higher tolerance for risk than others."

While the statement is true, it seems to me in this and other instances it sidesteps the onerous task of learning the lesson which, as human history illustrates, is quintessential human behavior. This dynamic is succinctly summed up by Kurt Vonnegut's response to the well known George Santayana insight, "Those who cannot remember the past are condemned to repeat it."

"I've got news for Mr. Santayana: we're doomed to repeat the past no matter what. That's what it is to be alive."

As a species, as a culture, as a lifestyle, as members of communities of skiers, mountaineers, firemen, housewives, school teachers, politicians, writers, sky divers, bartenders, bankers, clergy, drug addicts and thieves we are, as the great Vonnegut noted, doomed to repeat the past. That is what it is to be alive. The silver lining in being alive is that as individuals we are sometimes capable of learning, sometimes without even remembering the past, much less having to repeat its mistakes. As a group, any group—any group—that capability is not so evident.

There are always those individuals in every adventure and aspect of life who stand out from the group by their ability to learn the lesson, gain the insight, raise the standard and in some small or large way expand the limits of the possible by example. Sometimes these individuals learn from their own egregious mistakes, sometimes they learn without them.

(The skier mentioned earlier who jumped off the cliff onto a loaded steep slope reportedly told a good friend, "That will never happen again." Good for him, the individual who learned.) Usually, those who raise the standards become the stars, the leaders, the ones to emulate and, eventually, exceed. They become the beacon and the authority, and they do not last long. It has been only 60 years since Tensing Norgay and Edmund Hillary became the first humans to climb Everest, a milestone in mountaineering and human endeavor. Now any person with $60,000, a modicum of fitness and the desire for a piece of the action can climb Everest. My old friend Yuishiro Miura, who climbed Everest when he was 70 years old and again when he was 75, climbed it again at the age of 80. A couple of weeks before this writing Ueli Steck, arguably the finest climber in the world at the moment, and his two climbing partners were attacked by an angry mob of a hundred Sherpas whose profession involves getting those $60,000 clients up the mountain. The Sherpas were angered by a perceived violation of 'etiquette' on the part of the climbers.

Risk tolerance and etiquette delineate boundaries and, like fences, create good neighbors. When they are crossed some of the dynamics of accidents and high achievement in the mountains and elsewhere come a bit more into focus. I will argue (admittedly without having been there) that Steck's personal experience, focus, knowledge and unusual skill provide him a risk tolerance and security for both himself and those around him not available to any of the professional Sherpas who were so offended by and, according to reports, violent toward him and his climbing mates. Sherpas do not and should not be expected to understand that, unlike the intention of etiquette, risk tolerance is not democratic. For Sherpas, Everest is for clients, not climbers, and one ignores that cultural reality according to one's own tolerance for risk. Ho ho.

In an age when personal and professional spraying and promotion via films, I phones, the internet, GoPros, You Tube and Facebook are both immediate and endemic to the mountain culture, the latest exploit of the standard bearers, the super stars and the icons of the edge is immediately known and available to the world. The levels of achievement and risk tolerance of every super star of the mountains, seas, plains and cities in history are connected to and built upon the efforts of their respective communities. But those levels, no matter how well sprayed and promoted to the general populace, are only available to a few. Just because one sees a film of someone jumping off a cliff onto a steep slope and carving great turns in powder does not mean that every other similar mountain slope will not slide. Every slope, like very person, is different. The reasons for this are complex and obvious and, for some, difficult to accept and impossible to learn. As the good Kurt observed, we are as a species doomed to repeat the past. As individuals we can make some progress.

The level of risk tolerance for, say, Ueli Steck, Alex Honnold, Shaun White, Kristen Ulmer, Will Gadd and others who came before and more who will follow, is different in both kind and degree from those of less commitment and effort, mountain intelligence and instinct, attention to detail and that indefinable quality that some are born with and most are not that can be polished and enhanced but never earned. It can be called 'genius' but might be nothing more than having been born with better vision or hand/foot-eye coordination than others. However one chooses to define it, that quality keeps some alive in mountains where others perish. As standards move up so do expectations, personal and cultural, but in all things there are only a few capable of living on or close to the edge. None of them can live there for very long, time being as relative as levels of risk tolerance. And when the many push to where only the few can, with luck, survive there will be accidents remarkably similar to those in the past.

Jason's insight is always worth keeping in mind. That is, always listen to yourself—not the herd, not the promotion, not the cameraman, not the super star, not the comparison, certainly not the expert or authority—just yourself, your trusted friend who is the only one who can differentiate between wanting and thinking you should want to. Only you know what a tolerable risk is for you, and usually, not always, that risk is made more dangerous to the degree that it is comparative.

PART FOUR

Climbing Fiction

CHAPTER TWENTY-TWO

The First Ascent of Olympus Mons

a delayed report from Mars

Story by Andrew Acro

ONLY NOW that the 300-year energy war has run out of energy am I free to report on a most unusual achievement in mountaineering history, the first ascent of Olympus Mons, the highest mountain yet climbed in the Free Solar System.

Man had set foot on top of Olympus Mons before our climb of the 24,120-meter-high Gargantuan, three times as high as Earth's Everest and with a base 600 kilometers across, as wide as California's Pacific Cesspool Boulevard is long and in fact man was there while we climbed. But until our expedition, every person had gotten to the top by personnel carrier, usually electromagnetic or nuclear powered, though a few craft with more modern propulsion systems had been used. The experimental Transcend I, the telepathic-powered craft that had mysteriously crashed near the summit crater of the mountain early in the year 2281 was such a vehicle. This crash, now ten years ago, is most pertinent to our story.

It started for me about six months after the Transcend I crashed. I had been living normally, that is, climbing around the world, getting by any old way; working as little as possible; and, whenever I could hoard enough wealth, escaping to one of the three non-city refuges on earth. I had been to all three, but preferred the Sahara to either of the poles. My reputation as a mountaineer was spreading, bringing in a few televideo contracts and a wealthy client or two.

Like most of my climbing friends, I had avoided learning any skills useful to the military (or so I thought). But I had gained a name attached to skill by making the first unprotected ascent of the 1200-meter glass-covered Transgalactic Computer Building in uptown Moab; and I had put up the first-ever 5.18 on Uranus Wall inside the Shasta Nuclear Mistake Shelter, a little gem I called "A General's Game for Drones," done before the time after the Liverless Nuclear Breeder succumbed to passion and made life unlivable on the surface of Earth for two years, a time every person who lived through it remembers. With my friend Sheffield Stamp I'd climbed Everest from the bottom of the Northeast Face and made it down to the South Col Hotel in time for dinner. And the final blow was all the publicity after I snuck into Diznee City for the Senile in the old Yosemite Gully and soloed the big Captain Cliff in less than 20 minutes. I would have pulled it off with no trouble if some old woman at the 1000-meter level of the Tissyack Towers hadn't spotted me from the window of her retirement cell and called the military goons. They charged me with disobedience to the Law of Off-Limit Territory, Trespassing on the Right of the Elderly Rich to Have an Unchanging View, and Lack of Repentance for a Crime Well Done.

I was in deep trouble, but after five days of dark detention in the cellar of Curry Compound I was suddenly released.

I thought my climbing reputation and public opinion—after all, climbing doesn't hurt anyone except, sometimes, the climber, and that's his or her affair—were responsible for my release. In a way I'd never anticipated, I was right. Harry Hopper had gotten me out, and he was waiting for me outside.

Like most everyone I knew who Harry was, but I'd never met him. Now that he's been appointed to a high cabinet position in the Solar Republic of Universal Justice, it is no longer a secret that he worked for many years as a secret agent for the CYA (Check Your Act) of the Free Solar System, using his mountaineering interests and exploits as cover for some very bizarre adventures. None of these was stranger than ours, an episode in the classic CYA tradition of mountaineering espionage begun on Earth's Himalaya range in the twentieth century, not long before greed for that exhausted mineral substance called "oil" started the energy war in a place called the Near East on Earth. But our effort was more successful than those early endeavors.

Harry stood alone and waved the goons away. The jerks. They disappeared.

"Hello, Andrew," he said jovially, extending his hand as if we were old friends.

"You know me?" I asked, suddenly suspicious and alert.

"Of course, Andrew; we all know you. You're one of the great osmiridium men of mountaineering."

I blushed.

"Come," he continued. The thin face atop the slight body quit smiling, and his gray-green eyes bored through me. "We don't have time for idle talk." He glanced around the empty steel yard. "We're going to Mars," he whispered.

"We are? Whatever for?"

"We'll talk later."

Three hours later we were gathered, five of us, in the locked conference patio of Pan Earth's daily rocket shot to Planetia, the largest Martian colony and the only reason the entire solar system had not fallen to the enemy. The other three, all friends of mine from climbing, shared my surprise and bewilderment as to why we were suddenly on our way to Mars. None of us, except Harry, had ever been off our planet of birth. I was delighted to see Sheffield Stamp, my closest friend and climbing companion. He'd been atom-coptered out of the Manhattan Intrication where he had been found showing a favorite client some prime jungle wilderness climbing.

"Am I happy to see you," Sheff said, giving me a warm hug. "I don't know what this is about, but I'm glad we're together."

"Me too. This whole thing makes my testicles tighten."

Jeremiah Jefferson was there too. Jeremiah, a huge man with an easy smile and a legendary climbing and social reputation, had quit climbing four years earlier, to devote his life to spreading the cause of the Witnesses of the Apocalyptic Presence.

"Andrew Acro," Jeremiah said, his smile full of warmth and confidence. When are you going to settle down and make something of yourself?"

"As soon as you quit preaching that rocket exhaust you're always talking about and get back to climbing where you belong," I retaliated. He laughed and nearly broke my hand in his grip. Jeremiah's ideas were full of folly but I liked the man enormously. His climbing abilities are and were worthy of reverence, if, that is, you understand climbing.

The other member of our group was Merlin Macropsia, a quiet, reserved fellow at the height of his climbing powers, which were considerable. In the climbing world, Merlin was liked, respected, sought out as a climbing mate, and highly admired; but Merlin is a true-believing total devotee of the Church of Later Innocents of Ecumenical Saints, and I, for one, could never be at ease with him. His religious posture is that there are two kinds of people: those in the church who are salvaged, and those on the outside, who need salvaging. If they don't get salvaged by Merlin's church they get to the other side of innocence and are lost forever. So, friendly and kind and warm and intelligent as Merlin could be, I knew he viewed me as salvageable material. I wish to state publicly that I am not.

"Andrew," he said, "I've wanted to congratulate you for the Transgalactic coup. I admired that climb enormously. You have, you know, unlimited potential as a person. You can be anything you want to be."

He smiled so sincerely that I felt almost, but not quite, guilt, that feeling barely known anymore, a holdover from ancient times. But I knew he was telling me his feelings, and at any judgment Merlin was a dark force of a climber. I'd climb anywhere with him.

"Enough, enough," Harry broke in, "we've got work to do. And besides," his sly grin instilled in me a prudent feeling "you're undoubtedly a microspeck urined on because you're here without really any choice in the matter."

"You could say that, Harry, you refugee from penis envy," Jeremiah jumped into the gap. "Why have you arrested me and put me on a rocket to Mars? I don't, you politician, have any need or want for Mars."

"I understand your feelings," Harry said, clearly agitated, "but listen me out."

"Why?"

"Because you have no choice."

"Good edge," Jefferson conceded.

"Thank you," Harry continued. "You are, as the saying goes, probably wondering why we're gathered here together."

We all laughed, especially Harry. Somehow it felt better, understanding that no matter what was going on we were all in it together. Nevertheless, we threw every extra seat cushion at him.

"Enough." Harry grew swiftly serious. "Here's why we're here. You have never known this, but I work for the CYA and.......ahhhh......so do you, now. Starting from the time you were picked up until the time we return to Earth, you will be paid two weeks' living expenses for each day, plus bonuses if we're successful. What we're going to do is climb Olympus Mons, which you've all heard of, to do a bit of...ahhhh... official CYA work at the summit. And, if all goes according to plan, we'll have a personnel carrier ride back down. Now, you will remember hearing that the Transcend I crashed on Olympus Mons several months ago. I won't go into details; but the craft's developers are positive that something interfered with its flight, that it didn't crash through its own failure. Investigation found nothing. Then Allison Alpert, one of our best clairvoyants, was taken to Mars. Alpert insists that there is a Detectostroy unit somewhere on the top of Olympus Mons.

"We can't figure out how it got there, if it is there. Every craft sent out to investigate has discovered nothing. Still, Alpert insists it's there. If true, this would explain several setbacks we've suffered recently in this ageless war, losses truly embarrassing to us in the face of increasing opposition to the war.

"As you know, the war began before our time over the extinct substance called oil. The war's present critics, who argue that since the war was about the ownership rights of something no longer in existence, and who further try to find a reason in such nonsense to stop the war, well, such people obviously can't grasp the reason for the war. I can tell you these critics are cowardly and unreasonable and de facto supporters of the other side, but they are a nuisance and troublesomely free in thought and voice and action. In short, an embarrassment to the Free Solar System.

"Many times recently the enemy has anticipated precisely the movements of entire fleets of our war craft leaving Mars, and we've lost tens of thousands of craft and hundreds of skilled technicians. Not only is this a danger to our cause, it is a source of fuel to our critics, who are too stupid to realize that some of them must die in war in order for the rest of them to have jobs to support themselves and our great system.

"Now, as to Olympus Mons. We think there are two possibilities: either the other side has infiltrated some minds in our highest commands, or there is a vanishing Detectostroy unit operating from Olympus Mons. Or, perhaps, both. So, my friends and fellow climbers," Harry smiled brightly and something inside my mind slowly rolled over, "we have developed a theory. And we have the privilege of testing it."

He looked intently at each of us. "The theory is that there's a Detectostroy unit up there. The unit relays information to the other side. It monitors all craft movement on Mars, and is somehow able to detect conventional craft approaching Olympus Mons. It then vanishes. The Transcend I, because of its unique new propulsion system, was not detected in time for the unit to hide itself. Caught in the open with its detect apparatus exposed, the unit maser froze the Transcend I's force field before it could take evasive action or even transmit the information, and so the craft crashed. All the evidence supports this theory."

I liked this business less and less. The CYA, the worst pollutants in the system. War. Mars. The possibility of death. No, I did not like it.

"So," Harry went on, "to summarize, this unit is on top of Olympus Mons, able to detect any approaching craft, able to disappear and able to destroy any craft if necessary."

"But it can't detect the approach of the unaided human body," Jeremiah blurted out.

"Brilliant, Jeremiah," Harry said. "You've always had a fast mind. Technology, as usual, has forgotten to take into account the basics in this case, as in others, the human body."

"I don't want anything to do with this," Jeremiah said curtly.

"Take me back to the Curry Compound," I put in.

"Shit," said Sheff.

"My religion forbids me to engage in war, Harry," Merlin said softly.

"You don't have to fight, Merlin. All you are going to do is make the first ascent of the known universe's tallest mountain. Besides, all your religion forbids is the taking of other human life; if our theory is correct and if we are successful, we will save thousands of lives. And we will have done the biggest climb in history. Think of that. If we fail in our endeavor it will be for the glory of the Free Solar System."

Jeremiah and I looked and each other and shook our heads.

Harry," Sheffield pointed out, "in addition to being crazy, you've kidnapped us all."

"Yes, I know. In a free system we must sometimes remove freedom in order to retain freedom. *Everybody* knows that. Think about the climb."

We had plenty to think about. I recalled that Mars had been named by the ancients after their god of war, and that they had sacrificed human lives to gain his favor; its two worthless moons were named after the war god's attendants, Phobos and Deimos, Fear and Terror. I thought lots about those names and our situation during the three weeks it took to walk across the bizarre Martian landscape where, once Planetia is left, there are no buildings, the way it is said to have been on Earth in the time before memory began. Just sand and rocks. No vegetation. Interminable valleys and gullies and sometimes soil so fine you sink in up to your knees. All day long the wind blows hard. It blows red-orange dust into everything, into the creases of our self-contained enclosure suits, into any opening in our overflowing packs (which, with six weeks' supplies plus climbing gear, weighed well over 50 kilos each), and, worst of all, into our visor shields, clogging them so that it was necessary to continually clean them with anti-dust material. Nothing serious or difficult, just a never ending nuisance.

Besides the packs, our enclosure suits weighed some 23 kilos. These suits allowed liquid and food intake as well as waste product outtake. They recycled all urine and perspiration automatically, since we could not afford liquid loss. This took some psychological adjustment at first; but the system was quite sophisticated, and, as all mountaineers know, liquid to a tired body is more important than psychological preconceptions. Outdoor Martian defecation was something else. A series of electro-sealed flaps on the suit in the area of the buttocks enabled the wearer to create a mid-passage between his living space inside and the hostile environment. The flaps, called for some reason "grandpa flaps," worked like this: squat; open flap closest to body; defecate into second flap; close and seal first flap; open second flap to dump waste, which, because all liquids instantly vaporize in the thin atmosphere, immediately turns to powder; shake off and close second flap. The suits fully protected us from exposure to the 95 percent carbon dioxide atmosphere and the -125 C. temperature.

On Mars, gravitational pull is less and Earth-conditioned bodies can carry heavier loads, something prospective Martian climbers would do well to remember. Because of the thin atmosphere the famed 600-kph Martian winds are bearable, and probably easier than what we encountered near the summit of Everest in monsoon season.

Whenever the wind became dangerous we activated a special device used by geologists for field work on Mars, called a magneto-hold. Attached to the feet, hands and knees, the magneto-hold acts on the 16 percent iron content of Martian soil, riveting the climber to whatever piece of ground he is on. Given sufficient time, patience, and energy, *anything* on Mars can be climbed with a magneto-hold; but we used them only when safety warranted, which was often. To those Earth-bound climbers who will fault us for using such mechanical aids, I suggest they either try a 600-kpm wind or stuff it.

After the longest walk any of us had ever done, we began to climb. For a week previously Olympus Mons had been sticking up ahead of us, like another planet sitting on the one we were on. But, in all honesty, technical climbing as we know it is non-existent on Olympus Mons. Because of its lack of plate-tectonic activity in the planetary crust, the volcano that formed the mountain just kept adding to the same plume of lava; the slopes aren't all that steep, although they are certainly long. We did have to overcome a few 5.11 and 5.12 moves getting by crater rims and erosion gullies, but nothing we would have bothered hooking up for on Earth. Here, however, because of our unfamiliarity with the place, we were connected the entire time with nearly weightless but faultless one-millimeter carbon-fibered cord attached to our enclosure suite. We gained more than 3000 meters the first day, slogging through sand that had the consistency of heavy powder snow. Hard work, but we were conditioned from the approach. A nice little crater served for our first camp on the mountain. We had some excess liquid for emergency and depletion, but mostly we depended on our recycling systems. One doesn't climb for the purpose of ego-palate gratification, and we ate the standard ten-gram high-nutrition tablet for each meal, one per meal. It was sufficient. Our bodies had what they needed, though our egos had a hard time of it.

When it was dark we lay down, adjusted enclosure suit temperature and oxygen control, and slept. The soil particles in the atmosphere produced some spectacular color shows in the twilight; and it was pleasant to watch them in the last waking minutes of the day, the fiery spectacle of unavoidable life. We watched Phobos and Deimos in eclipse; we had seen them during the day as black spots crossing the sun. It was also interesting to see Phobos rise and set twice a day—very different from the single moon of Earth.

The second day saw us gain 5000 meters over variable terrain. The soil was sometimes as hard as granite, sometimes like knee-deep cottage cheese. That day we encountered two constant realities of Olympus Mons, both objectively and objectionably dangerous. First, the wind: it blows virtually all day but ceases at night, causing us to activate our magneto-hold devices more than we would have liked; often we could see only a few meters ahead. Second, Olympus Mons has a built-in defense that is far superior to any icefall, avalanche, rock fall, or fear factor of the most treacherous Earth mountain. The wind simply erodes away a part of the mountain, and whatever is left to gravity, say a boulder the size of hovercraft or a good-sized man, starts rolling down the mountain. After a few thousand meters it builds up quite a lot of speed. Because of the wind and the dust there's no advance warning and suddenly a dark object hurtles by at 100 kph and is gone. There's no defense. It's like crawling across a busy rocket landing pad in dense smog, hoping you'll reach the other side.

The truth is, in any other situation I've known I would have turned around. But the CYA's long reputation, dating at least back to shortly before the beginning of the war when the Third Metric World statesman Alberto Yende was murdered in his own office by CYA functionaries was enough to make the four of us realize that Harry was not your usual mountaineering expedition chief. We were climbing for our lives, in more than the usual sense.

The CYA, it is now known, got the war started: its employees raided certain desert oil deposit encampments, killed all the technicians there, and unsuccessfully attempted to destroy the oil-mining machinery, while disguised as members of the other tribe in that area than the one in whose territory the oil reposed. The CYA counted on the centuries-old, marrow-deep hatred between the two tribes living in that area to present the incident as an excuse to fight, and it did. Over the years the entire known universe lined up on the side of one or the other of those tiny desert tribes whose original names only the scholar remembers. They were, literally, destroyed by their own hatreds. Yet the war continued. Well, that's how the CYA works, and we knew that if we wanted out of this one alive we'd have to do a good job. Also, we lacked enough supplies to reverse the walk. This knowledge and circumstance somewhat dulled the joy and the sense of adventure normally felt while undertaking unsolved mountaineering problems.

Our progress slowed. The wind continued. The need to constantly attach to the mountain with magneto-hold, the sense of helpless fear that came over us with each passing/hurtling/lethal eroded-away piece of Olympus Mons, the pure size of that unbelievable hulk, slowed us down.

The days flowed into each other. There were just us and that seemingly endless mountain with its red and orange and black and yellow and brown rock and deep black lava, its daytime red/yellow/ orange dust storms, and the peaceful nighttime views of the moons of

Mars and other stars and planets. The mountain had ledges, plateaus, steep sections and gradual ones; but the overriding feeling it gave us was endlessness. Olympus Mons, the endless mountain.

Harry, the weakest climber, urged us to push on at all times when both fatigue and intelligence indicated otherwise. After all, fatigue clouds judgment, and life can be terminated just as quickly and surely by falling off non-technical terrain as off the smoothest glass building. Harry's continued disregard for our opinions contributed to the resentment we carried.

Jeremiah, typically, though he had "retired" from climbing four years before, was so enthusiastic, so excited to be doing what he loves to do, that he continually sided with Harry. Push on! Push on! I called them the Excelsior Twins, after a verse ancient even before the war began.

On one of those indistinguishable days, though none of us can recall precisely, we encountered an eroded cliff, with an interesting chimney caused by some geologic power of nature we do not yet understand. It was unanimously agreed that I should climb it, leaving a line for the others.

Without using my magneto-hold, I spent the best two hours of the climb working up the 700 meter chimney. It was exhilarating climbing. It would have been exceedingly simple on Earth, but under the circumstances, and considering my enclosure suit and pack, it was quite interesting. I could have used a laser beam to drill holes in the rock for secure protection hooks, but we were exceedingly paranoid about detection and had agreed to use this only as a last resort. So I fell back on a barely remembered system perfected by some ancients in a place that is now part of the island of London that used to be called Wales. In this system, the climber protects himself by placing loops of line around irregularities in the climbing surface, or by putting tiny and irregular pieces of metal into holes and cracks in the rock and clipping the climbing line into a line attached to the metal. It's scary at first but works marvelously well. (Not all the ancients were as stupid as the present state of Earth makes them appear.)

Fortunately, no falls occurred to test the system. At one point I smiled and then laughed at myself. What irony that the CYA the ancient order of deceit and manipulative violence that represents everything I wanted my life not to mean had finally found a way to use the only skills I'd allowed myself to develop.

I broke out of the chimney to be met by the wind. I activated my magneto-hold and tied off the line so the others, saving time and energy, could climb it with the classic ascendeurclamps, attached to hands and feet. A small crater offered good protection. I felt wonderful, satisfied with climbing and very happy.

We bivouacked in the crater. One by one as my mates came up the classic expedition strains began to show. Macropsia and Hopper got into a heated argument about our pace. We were all fatigued, and getting tired of ten-gram nutritional tablets for subsistence. The strangeness of the climb with its peculiar defenses, just being on Mars, the underlying fears of what we would find on top, had thinned our cooperative abilities. By the time we bedded down, my sense of well-being after climbing the chimney had dissipated.

In the morning we were all irritable, sluggish, and inattentive. We started climbing up a moderately steep slope of loose soil in which we sank to the knees. I was climbing second behind Harry. Before the wind came up we saw a cliff band several thousand meters above, beyond which we could not see. When the wind descended the dust obscured everything. We toiled upward. Wind. Dust. Labor. And then it seemed like the mountain just came up and hit me in the face, and we both started moving. Suddenly I was knocked off my feet and rolling end over end, completely buried under sand, rocks, and dirt in motion. My pack was ripped from my back. There was no color, only blackness and movement and rocks banging against my enclosure suit.

My mind dwelt on the suit, for breaking it would mean the end of existence. I was falling, rolling, being pushed by an avalanche of Martian soil; and then the line came taut and it felt like I was being broken in half. The avalanche roared over me and under me and pulled at me to join it. Then it was over, as quickly as it had begun, and everything was silent and dark.

The next thing I knew Merlin and Jeremiah were digging me out and shouting for me to wake up. I have never known such gratefulness as came over me when I saw them, but there was no time to indulge in personal emotions.

"Andrew, Andrew," yelled Merlin, "c'mon. Wake up. We've got to dig out the others. Are you all right?"

"Yes, I'm okay," I lied. I felt like going to sleep. My body raged against me as I stood up. The line disappeared into the soil, and we immediately set to work uncovering it. In an hour we had retrieved the other two, and I still think it was what the ancients called a miracle that we all survived. Sheff and I just hugged each other wordlessly when we uncovered him.

We figured out what must have happened: a huge section of the cliff band we'd seen in the morning had collapsed in the middle and rushed down the mountain and hit us. As it worked out, the break in the cliff created by the collapse gave us an easy passage through; but both Sheff and I had lost our packs, with all our food, climbing equipment, extra liquid, weapons, and repair material for the enclosure suits. The only reason all of us weren't swept away by the slide is that Merlin, who happened to be last on the line, somehow saw what was happening and had time to activate his magneto-hold. Only that held us to the mountain. Good old Merlin. He must live right.

Our position was not good. Merlin and Harry began to argue. Harry wanted to move on as soon as we dug him out. I wanted to stop and rest. My body ached, my mind was numb, and my spirit was looking for a place to land. Jeremiah was surly and uncommunicative. Sheff and I were both concerned about where losing our packs had left us in terms of supplies.

"Blast you, Harry," Sheff said, jumping into Merlin's argument. "Look what you've done to us! We could die up here, and if something happens to you none of us has the faintest idea of how to get out. And... and...Harry, you...are...an...asshole!"

The enormity of what he'd said hit my old friend the way a cat baps a mouse around; and, believe it or not, all of us started laughing, gut-hysterical laughter, until we were all on the ground paralyzed with the one shred of humor in our situation.

"You sly bastard, Harry," Jeremiah finally managed.

"Now I want you guys to take real good care of me. You hear?" Harry said, and we all howled, especially Harry.

It was easy to see how Hopper had managed to rise as high as he had in this life; and, strangely enough, the strains eased up. Even the unethical side of life can be made understandable and, therefore, funny.

We continued upward. Our enclosure suits had been tough enough not to tear during the avalanche and kept us from the classic Earthly altitude and breathing problems, but after four weeks of pushing as hard as possible our endurance was low. So was our capacity to believe in much outside of putting one foot in front of the other.

On what we later determined was the eleventh day of climbing, Sheff suddenly pointed out that we were almost to the top. Indicative of the state of our minds was our surprise that we were actually near the summit. Harry called us together for a conference and then we moved fast. When we estimated that we were only a few hours from the rim where we could, at last, look out across the 70 kilometer-wide extinct volcano crater that is the summit of Olympus Mons, we stopped. We would go to the summit under cover of darkness. As Harry said to us, "I have no more idea than you what we'll find there."

When it was dark we set out. Fear and Terror, like evil's own lanterns, crossed the sky, and our minds. The going was not difficult, and Deimos gave off enough light for fair visibility. Since there is less wind on Mars at night the visibility was in some ways better than during the day. Perhaps night climbing is the future of Martian mountaineering. We pushed on over easy ground.

And then, suddenly, it was done. There just wasn't any mountain left. We silently shook hands all around. Then, according to the plan, we found a good crater to hide in and await the dawn. To say that we were apprehensive is an injustice to the power of the god of war and his attendants. Give me a good, old-fashioned, dangerous, ridiculous, scary, non-socially-redeeming climb any day over waiting for daylight on the top of Olympus Mons.

The first light found us peering over the crater rim with high-powered teleoptics. Nothing: sand; rocks; a huge dead basin. After about three hours of motionless observation I was beginning to succumb to boredom when a most startling event occurred. Less than a kilometer away on the rim a boulder about the size of a large hovercraft opened in the middle and two men in enclosure suits stepped out. It was one of the strangest moments of my life.

"Holy exhaust," I whispered, despite our agreement of silence.

Harry's head swiveled toward me like a detect unit picking up an incoming irreversible reaction missile, Harry and everybody else. They saw where my teleoptic was pointed and followed. To the two men we watched, of course, the thought that others might be watching them was completely absent. In a way it was great voyeuristic fun. They were, we understood after a time, getting their daily exercise, much needed as it turned out, for they had been living in cramped quarters inside that "rock," the most elaborately equipped and camouflaged Detectostroy unit Harry had ever seen. An hour's gambol on the highest rim of Olympus Mons each morning was the highlight of their existence and nearly the extent of their movement. The two of them ran around the "boulder," wrestled, took advantage of the low Martian gravity to do front and back flips for each other's scrutiny, and, all in all, acted like two six-year-old boys during rest break from state educational torture sessions. They held our undivided and silent attention for an hour.

"Well, I'll be Hitlered, Nixoned, and Crucified," Harry muttered. "One of those technicians is Cary Catalin."

"Who's he?" said Merlin.

"One of my boys. I trained him in all the basics."

"Basics of what?" Jeremiah asked.

"The basics of our profession," Harry answered with a solemn dignity. He seemed genuinely hurt by Catalin's conversion.

"Looks like he missed one or two of them," Merlin commented.

The two men finally ceased their independence and returned to their boulder which closed behind them and just sat there like the boulder it wasn't. After a few minutes several scanner-antennae moved out from the boulder's surface, to be joined by an obvious maser beam launcher. Harry's theory had proved sound.

We spent the next five days in a continuous watch on the boulder. There were only those two technicians with the unit and every morning at the same time they exited the unit and took their daily exercise. The rest of the time they monitored the movement of craft on Mars.

On the morning of the sixth day we ended it. We were waiting for Catalin and his mate when they came out for exercise. Their astonishment rendered them temporarily paralyzed. That, along with the menacing aim of Harry's laser gun, made them quite submissive. We took over the cleverly disguised Detectostroy unit. Our mission was accomplished.

True to his word, Harry got us back to Planetia. We were all handsomely rewarded, and each of us was given the Free System Legion of Merit award. I am in no way qualified or motivated to report what significance our climb had in the effort to end the war, but after we took it over the unit was used to relay false information to the other side. Also, the vindication of the Transcend I and, therefore, the usefulness of telepathic power caused research in that field to be expanded. As everyone now knows, telepathic power is drawn from an unlimited and nonmaterial source, and is not based on something that can be possessed or, finally, fought over. We ended 300 years of energy war misery last year by giving the other side, in exchange for peace, access to more energy than has ever been fought about in the entire history of the known universe.

So, despite my personal aversion to war and warriors, I feel our climb was a worthwhile accomplishment, both for climbing and for the free system in general. 24,000-meter-high mountains offer new dangers and challenges, and I emphasize to future climbers of the extreme the importance of adjusting the scale of the possible within each human mind as the safest, surest method of being equal to these new challenges. Under the unique situation that brought us to Olympus Mons, we did not have the time and the understanding to do that. I realize now that we had a large measure of that essence many people these days think is only an ancient superstition—luck.

CHAPTER TWENTY-THREE

The Descent

THE SUMMIT WAS NOT AS EXPECTED but Erik Austin had climbed to the top, a mound on a snow-blasted ridge. The world below and all of humanity were obscured by clouds. "The summit," he said aloud. "I made it." There was neither view to savor nor companion to share. Feelings of accomplishment and self-congratulation, like the summit itself, were not as he had anticipated, but such chimeras no longer surprised nor disappointed him. Expectation and memory had proven unreliable and he was not anticipating or reviewing for correction ... anything. There was nothing more to climb. He was left with the unexpected present moment, alone on the summit of a ridge of snow just above the clouds with nowhere to go outside of right now. Empty and full, impervious and satisfied in the same breath, he looked up at blue sky and sun and down into the rising clouds with crisp attention and appreciation of their combined beauty. After a few minutes he smiled a silent farewell to the summit and began the descent.

"What am I going back to?" he asked with the first step down. "I wanted to reach the summit at any cost and now I have and there's nothing here except me. Nothing here except me and me and snow and clouds below and me and I can't stay here and it's a long way back." With his usual discipline he focused on the present task of getting off the mountain, one step, one move, one breath at a time. He was comfortable with the single move in a chosen direction guided by implacable concentration that had always kept him a step ahead of.....

what? How can you go back and stay a step ahead? Back to his beautiful wife and two lovely children who filled him with love and happiness and meaning? His students at the University who brought him purpose and satisfaction as he helped them discover their better selves and grow into their own minds? His sufficient material well being? His considerable fame? Was he going back a step ahead of them all? Why? No step can be ahead of itself, he thought, and he had just finished the hardest step of all. Or had he? The wind-blasted snow of the ridge was hard. Each cramponed step was placed with unrelenting precision and a momentum that had propelled him through life, up countless climbs and mountains and through fierce storms that defeated and too often killed unwary and unlucky companions Now, finally, he had reached the summit of the hardest, most inaccessible of them all, a mound on a high ridge where nothing lives for long. In leaving the summit he felt austerity and improbable accomplishment falling behind. It was the first time he was in step with himself, neither ahead nor behind. It is an unaccustomed feeling. Here is where I am, he thought. Here. How obvious. Here is where I am. Here is where I have always been and will always be. Right here. Not a step ahead nor a step behind on the way to somewhere else. Right here is the only step there is. What a thought! The only move is the one you are making. The only step is right here and now. There is no there or then. Erik remembered the phrase but not its source, "There is no there there." He smiled with weary happiness and an image of his family entered his mind and he felt their unseen, material presence. There is here here, he thought. Not hear hear. Here here.

Without wind it was strangely still. The sound of crampon biting snow, the soft fabric of clothes and pack rubbing and the labor of each breath seemed intrusions on silence. The sun, high in the bright sky on top, quickly faded with the descent into clouds and he soon missed visual clarity in the diminishing light. Weary from effort and the physiological struggle of living where no creature can live for long, his thoughts strayed to the momentary summit's fleeting crispness of vision from a mound of snow that was not as he had imagined. He watched his mind jump back to the summit and forward to base camp and further forward to home and back again to the summit in the space of only a few steps. Then he caught his mind and anchored it to the present, carefully placed step and the effort of each breath. Erik was very tired and he was pleased when after a time of attentive descending he reached the top of the Great Notch, the weakness, the key, the only access to the ridge that led to the summit. His mind shifted again from here to a summit of blue sky and beauty and perfection that seemed a thousand years past, an experience from a different life, as he stepped with incomplete attention to the movement of the moment on a six inch wind ridge of snow that crumbled under his right crampon. Erik lost balance 20 feet short of the break in the cornice he had climbed on the ascent, and the short drop of impact triggered a collapse of the entire cornice. He fell with it like a street drunk in the most neglected city of humanity, dropping down the snow-filled couloir of the Great Notch faster than thought could return from a past moment of less substance than a dream, accompanied by suitcase-sized blocks of snow that hit him as hard as failure. A step ahead? He felt more anger at his lapse of attention than fear of its possible consequences. That was his way, anger conquering fear, an unexamined credo of perseverance in the face of an unexamined, inextinguishable dread of inadequacy. Every effort to satisfy or alleviate the fear vanished into the emptiness of ending each effort. In Erik Austin's life fear and the struggle to banish it were like a snake eating its own tail.

Cobra-calm rage masked his deepest fears and was his first response to every disappointment, obstacle and mistake. He willed himself to rise from the collapsing snow, but personal volition has no foundation in a fall and his resolve vanished. There was no control and fear and anger were replaced by the emptiness of limitation and circumstance. Time slowed as it can in crisis and he noted that both recent summit and immediate future descended with him into the clouds along a reversal of the path of his past. He was abruptly informed, even amused, by the joint companionship of high accomplishment and unexpected falls. The other summits of his life had always abandoned him, or, perhaps, he abandoned them for the next one, but this summit was coming with him and he would need no other. There was no room for anger or recrimination in the fatigue-filled emptiness. His body slammed into the snow, flipped and accelerated again and he thought of Jake and saw Jake's face as he plummeted down the couloir that was the Great Notch.

On the first attempt it had been Jake who found the Great Notch, a solitary unobvious breach in the enormous wall below the ridge. When Erik first saw the wall in person it was as different from the photographs as word is from deed and his confidence shifted like the whuumping sound of a breaking cornice. There were sudden vibrations in determination. He was wary. His practice in times of doubt was to obscure qualms and fear of failure with physical movement and a demeanor of confidence that masked a wider range of emotions. The tactic served him well and had often kept him going when most of his companions wanted to retreat. On that first expedition only Jake came with him as far as the basin below the enormous wall where they set up camp in the most isolated, wild, high place either had ever been. They cooked dinner and talked and agreed it was the mountain of all mountains and acknowledged the good fortune that had brought them to it. They were comrades if not close friends but their mutual respect for the other's mountain skills, intelligence and judgment was more valuable to each than the impalpable bonds of friendship. Jake told him that he would not have come so far and would have turned around with the rest of the expedition, if it weren't for Erik's persistence and obvious confidence. "You really inspired me," Jake said. What Jake perceived as confidence felt more like anger and fear of failure to Erik. Jake's sincerity was both stirring and instructive, but he was more embarrassed than flattered. That night it snowed, wind shook the tent, sleep was fitful. By morning the storm had passed and after two hours of cooking, eating, drinking, organizing gear, and dressing for high altitude climbing, the two began taking turns breaking trail through knee deep snow up a steep slope rising from basin to the huge, vertical, snow-blasted wall.

Jake was stronger that day. When Erik slowed after hours of effort Jake told him to take a break while he went ahead for "a little reconnaissance." He rested in the snow and watched Jake continue another hour to the base of the wall which rose over them like a massive wave frozen in place which, he mused, from a certain perspective of time, it was. He was neither fearful of failure, angry nor ambitious about anything. He was just extremely fatigued and his mind was quiet, clear, peaceful and uncharacteristically satisfied. He later contemplated that time sitting in the snow, having spent himself and contentedly having nothing more to give, nothing more to take, nothing more, nothing more, and he was not unhappy. That was the puzzler when he thought about it later. It wasn't his way to sit in the snow and accept that it was over. It was never over. There was always the next step, the next climb, next something.

But this one was over, the expedition done, he said to himself, watching Jake move along the great wall, first to the left and then back right where he paused in contemplation for several minutes. When Jake finally turned around and began descending Erik got up and descended to camp at the bottom of the basin and had hot food and drinks ready when Jake arrived. He was surprised and disoriented by Jake's enthusiasm and its sharp contrast to his own fatigue. "It goes, it goes," Jake insisted, describing the break in the great wall that could not be seen from the basin, a not too steep snow-filled gully that appeared to reach the summit ridge. They ate and drank and huddled in the tent discussing options. They could rest a day and attempt the summit or retreat to catch up with the already retreating expedition. Jake wanted to try for the summit. Food supply was marginal, cumulative fatigue was significant and their support team was gone, but Jake wanted to try. It was one of the few times in a sterling and aggressive climbing career that Erik was the naysayer, listening to an instinctive wisdom stronger than ambition or the reason of odds. Erik prevailed and they retreated to try another day.

Five years later Jake was dead and he had reached the summit alone and was descending from the ultimate peak, the hardest of them all. Before leaving home he had promised himself and his family and his students and even the memory of Jake that he would never leave again after this last, ultimate step, the most difficult of them all.

Sliding falling flipping hitting snow accelerating slowing rolling scraping banging banging snow everywhere for what seemed a long time before slowing slowing to no motion or sound. Silence for a time and then the staccato noise of his lungs sucking in air and coughing it out with uninhibited desperation. Erik's body hurt. He did not move or open his eyes which were squeezed shut in a last line of defense. He listened to his lungs and tried to feel his body, but only an unfamiliar sound and an ancient cold responded. He was lying on his left side and had fallen down the entire couloir as the terrain was nearly flat. He wanted to go to sleep. Nothing would feel as good as sleep, but, instead, he opened his eyes. He closed them after a few moments because what he saw was not what he should have seen. He opened them again and what he should not have seen was still there and he regarded it carefully. His fall down the couloir of the Great Notch had left him at the top of the basin about 50 feet from the base of the huge rock wall that rose above him like a wave, and clearly visible in the rock before him was the outline of a door.

Erik closed his eye. When he opened them again the door was still visible.

He sat up and his body hurt but it worked. He flexed his feet and hands and shrugged his shoulders and did not take his eyes off the door. He decided against trying to stand up and crawled toward the door without questioning the incongruities of action, intended destination or what he was seeing. When he was ten feet from the door it opened and he stopped moving. A barely perceptible sweet, floral aroma rode into his nostrils on the first warm air they had breathed since leaving sleeping bag and tent late the night before. As he stood up and moved to the door a sharp blast of cold wind blew from the summit along the wall and nearly knocked him down. Erik stepped through the door and it closed behind him.

His first sensation was that in the opening and closing of a door he had gone from unimaginable cold and peril to a warm, dependable world as beautiful and full of promise as the hearts of children. He removed his mittens, goggles, hood and hat, stuffed them inside his parka, and looked around in the semi-darkness with a comfortable feeling of familiarity as if he had visited this place before. He was standing on a platform at the top of a steep stairway that descended toward a warm, diffused light and the distant sounds of music and singing birds.

He began the descent. Though the staircase was steep and winding and suspended in space Erik felt secure and comfortable and noted that his breathing was normal and his body did not hurt. He descended without effort, as if clad in slippers and light clothes instead of boots and crampons and mountaineering gear. The light grew brighter and the sounds of life more distinct. As he came round a turn in the staircase three young women in light robes and an elderly, small man greeted him without speaking and beckoned for Erik to follow them down the stairs. He followed without question, strangeness or discomfort down winding, sometimes steep stairs into an empty space imbued with a soft red ambient light. He felt warm in body and comfortable with the women and the man. Soft yellow lights lit the stairway like tiny suns in a dark universe. Vines hung from what seemed a roof and foliage from a concealed forest shimmered in a soft wind and he saw two waterfalls cascading strangely out of sight. It was the most beautiful place Erik had ever seen and he noticed other descending staircases and looking up he saw that they rose into the innards of other mountains, other ranges, other worlds than the one he was in and the one he so recently had been descending.

His hosts beckoned for him to stand next to them and they told him to look at the birds he had been hearing and to listen to their music. The colorful and small birds were of a kind he had never seen, and they flew over a lush landscape of herbs, flowers, blossoms and grasses of many varieties. The man was short and thin with long silver hair and beard. His skin was the weathered, rough skin of a lifetime in cold wind, but he moved with an easy grace and his eyes twinkled and radiated warmth, intelligence and energy. He was dressed in loose wool pants that did not reach his ankles held up by suspenders over a thick pullover sweater. His feet were clad in sandals.

The three women wore diaphanous white robes hanging low from one shoulder and loosely tied with long gold sashes at the hip. One wore colored slippers, the others were barefoot. All three had light brown skin, and light blue eyes and dark, wavy brunette hair to their waists and

Erik thought they appeared to be sisters of a regal realm with voices as soothing as the sound of a gentle stream in the woods. The steepness of the stairs leveled and before long they reached a flat platform and the man told Erik to take what he wished from a large box on the platform and to put on more comfortable clothes. Erik found a soft robe and removed his mountaineering gear and when he donned the robe it massaged his skin and he felt instantly rejuvenated and strangely happy.

They left the platform and the sensation of having a floor beneath his feet vanished and Erik was suspended in space and able to move effortlessly with freedom and security. He followed his hosts and soon saw some oddly different people, like his hosts. Others were more familiar, as if they were members of a large base camp. Everyone he saw seemed happy and at ease, talking with each other, lounging about, many with a small drink in their hands. One of the women handed him a drink and told him to drink it. He asked her what her name was and she replied, "It doesn't matter, Erik. You will always recognize me."

"How do you know my name?" he asked.

She laughed softly and replied, "You could only be who you are, Erik, no one else. Sip your drink."

He did and it was a warm, sweet tea that infused him with energy. It was easy to breathe and move. He recalled how difficult breathing was before he entered the door and he felt fulfilled, suspended and secure. The three women and the man left him and he found a chair in a comfortable place to sit and observe the new environment, the people and the change in his own circumstance. He saw a fire and some large trees, grass and chairs scattered around. Birds and butterflies fluttered freely around some white horses and near the fire was a mountain lion stretched out asleep on its back. Erik did not feel threatened. The people were casually moving around or sitting in the chairs, conversing in small groups, and silently alone, Erik thought they seemed what he termed "an international mix" and everyone was content. So was he and it was wonderful to be content.

The woman who wore the colored slippers approached Erik, refilled his cup, smiled, sat down next to him and without introduction or a question began to explain what he was experiencing and observing.

"Everyone you see here was a climber like you. They were brought in out of the cold before they froze. Some of them had collapsed or had simply sat down to rest and fallen asleep. Others had gotten lost and confused. Many of them, like you, had fallen or been buried by snow slides and had only a short time to live. Most of them, the ones whose appearance is strange to your eyes, had already died. All of them had the choice of deciding to stay here or return to your world and resume their other lives. All of the ones you see here chose to remain and they will not climb again except in their dreams. They are, as you see, happy in this place where living requires no effort and time does not pass or, really, exist. Several of your old friends from your land are here and will be happy to see you if you make the decision to stay. And they are happy for you if you do not stay. Your friend Jake is here."

The woman with the light blue eyes and dark wavy hair leaned closer to Erik and looked carefully into his eyes. "Sometimes," she said, "people are only visitors here. Perhaps you are one of them. When visitors leave here they are filled with energy to be successful in their lives and future climbs in that other land, but they have the same difficulties and obstacles as before. When they descend into the denser air their memory of this place and these people is lost unless they return again. Sometimes they do. You are welcome to stay and you are free to leave. You have earned the freedom and joy of being here. The choice is yours, always yours."

Without another word, she leaned to Erik and kissed him full and sensuously on the lips. She smiled and got up and walked away to stand with the other people and he saw that they were all watching him, awaiting his decision.